Feline
Friends

EXISLE
PUBLISHING

Feline Friends

Tales from the heart

cat protection society
OF NSW INC.

CONTENTS

INTRODUCTION

Man domesticated the cat. And the cat, being a courteous creature, returned the favour.

—Anon

Jam took her own sweet time finding a home. A pretty female ginger tabby (only about a quarter of all ginger cats are girls) she'd come to Cat Protection as a stray mum. She raised her kittens with care and love and they all quickly found forever homes. She enjoyed life in our adoption centre. She was easygoing and relaxed, and loved the attention of volunteers and staff. She got on well with the other cats. So why was she with us for thirteen months?

The answer is some 10,000 to 12,000 years old: we didn't choose cats, they chose us. As it was then, so it is today, and thus Miss Jam would not make herself available or appealing to potential adopters ... until she found the people *she* wanted to live with.

Now known as Ginger Rogers, she enjoys a life of pleasant sophistication in the Sydney pied-à-terre of a couple who adore her. She found what she was looking for.

The development of agriculture is believed to have started around the Fertile Crescent (today's Middle East) about 12,000 years ago. Dogs had been companions of people before this; they had been domesticated and helped with hunting and protection, and didn't object to moving from place to place. When people progressed from hunting to agriculture and the storage of surplus grain, this attracted mice and their natural predators, cats.

Genetic studies show that all modern domestic felines are descendants of the species *Felis silvestris catus* ('cat of the woods') commonly known as a wildcat. There are five subspecies of wildcat — Sardinian (*Felis silvestris lybica*); European (*Felis silvestris silvestris*); Central Asian (*Felis silvestris ornata*); Sub Saharan African (*Felis silvestris cafra*); and Chinese Desert (*Felis silvestris bicti*). Look at any of these cats and it takes no imagination to picture them in front of a heater, purring. But while the Scottish Wildcat looks just like a large Mackerel Tabby, it is a true wild species (and protected as such).

The studies show that modern day moggies' strongest ancestral link is to the sub-species *Felis silvestris lybica*. This is interesting because it suggests that regional wildcats weren't locally domesticated but that the first domestic cats were 'exported' along with the skills of agriculture. Genetic evidence also reveals that those domestic cats didn't mind a fling with their new neighbours. This is no surprise to anyone who's lived with a cat — a domestic cat's wild side has never actually been tamed, it simply rarely reveals itself.

So there they were, *Felis silvestris lybica*, watching as people formed communities and stored the harvest, seeing the shelters being built and the warm fires being lit, and certainly not missing that very convenient food source (*Mus musculus*). As those people discovered the grain protection benefits of cats, the cats discovered the benefits of housing and human attention. Feline beauty was on their side: it's theorised that kittens' big eyes and snub noses evoke a nurturing response in people that's also biologically triggered by babies. The cats who adapted to living with people in human settlements thrived and their relatives are in our lounge rooms today.

Except for cats, all domestic animals are either herd or pack animals and were domesticated by people for a purpose, typically for food or labour. People could achieve this by taking on the alpha role in a pack or herd. Cats are social creatures but they do not rely on leadership for their survival as they are solitary hunters. It is this which makes the human–feline relationship unique and fascinating. Cats domesticated themselves and did not take orders, but thousands of years ago they forged a partnership with us that continues to this day.

It hasn't always been good for cats. While the ancient Egyptians worshipped them and the ancient Romans highly respected them, the nadir for cats' relationship with people came in Europe in the Middle Ages, when cats were persecuted as witches and agents of the devil. Cats were associated with paganism and threatened the power of the Church, and their destruction was not only unspeakably cruel but also so widespread their numbers were severely depleted. Of course, this allowed the rat population to explode and with it a wave of plagues that depleted the human population of Europe. When it was finally discovered that cats were helpful in reducing the plague, the relationship began to repair.

Ambivalence about cats is arguably rooted in the past. From reverence to superstition, people attributed supernatural powers to cats that a modern, educated person would reject. Yet there are many people who will still freely admit to an irrational dislike of cats.

Recent neurological studies have identified a specific area of the brain (the right amygdala) that reacts to and processes information about animals, suggesting they are a profoundly important part of human life. Perhaps centuries of fear and superstition about cats became hardwired for some people, or perhaps some people just need to dominate. Whatever it is, cats don't care. They'll do their own thing, make their own friends and always find people like us, who know that to be a part of this unique relationship is an honour and a joy.

This book is a celebration of the unique relationship between people and cats. The Cat Protection Society of New South Wales has been caring for cats — and the people who love them — since 1958. Over that time we've been witness to tens of thousands of cat-and-people stories: happy unions and reunions, and desperately sad losses and relinquishments. We've seen feline victims of vicious cruelty, and from time to time despaired at human character, but our faith is continually restored by the enormous generosity and kindness that so many are willing to give.

As in ancient times, the homeless cat has a knack for identifying those who will look kindly on them. The pregnant street cat always seems to choose a nice person's home under which to have her kittens. Whether they take her in or bring her to our shelter, she is cared for. And just like Jam (Ginger Rogers) she'll stay with us until she finds the right permanent home.

Cats won't stay with people who harm them, though sadly many trusting cats are the victims of obscene cruelty or neglect.

Ella came to our shelter in April 2007. A ladylike tortoiseshell, she'd been with us for year when she started limping. Her knee was badly affected by degenerative arthritis that could only be solved by amputating her leg. However, X-rays showed problems with her hips that meant she couldn't put pressure on them and so would not survive as a three-legged cat. Even with medication her pain was too much, and with many tears we made the decision for the vet to put her to sleep. The vet's opinion was that these problems had come about because she'd had an untreated injury earlier in her life; possibly she had been hit by a car.

As noted, cats aren't pack or herd animals but most are social (some cats, though, are definitely diva cats who demand to be the sole cat!). Ella was a gentle and maternal leader in the adoption centre. During her time with us she provided comfort and reassurance for newcomer kittens and cats alike. She especially took shy cats under her wing and would often share her sunny unit with feline friends for an afternoon snooze. This beautiful cat who had suffered so much in her past used her understanding to help other cats become confident. The afternoon we said goodbye to her a terrible silence came over the adoption centre room. Her room-mates mourned her and we joined them in their grief. It had been an honour to know her.

Cats do grieve — for people, for other cats, for dogs. They have rich emotional lives and while we can't communicate perfectly with them, one of the joys of living with cats is trying to learn their language.

Tinkerbell

Tinkerbell was a cat who came to us in grief because her owner had died. Tinkerbell was deaf so she couldn't hear the sound of her own mourning but all of us could (and probably our neighbours too). The sound was not just loud but heartbreaking. Communicating with cats is a challenge at the best of times but made even more so when the cat is deaf. We persevered and she finally came to settle down and found some comfort in the routines of life in our shelter. When she was adopted and had her own home with a very attentive and sensitive person, she positively blossomed.

Our cats come to us from all kinds of circumstances and we do our best to understand them and their needs, and to help match them with the right human companions. Often they will make friends with other cats in our care and some become so strongly bonded we will then only re-home them as a pair. Likewise the people we deal with each have their own stories, and increasingly we are seeing more cats surrendered because people are not allowed to keep them. This creates heartache for the person and for the cat, and it also denies the person the many benefits of pet ownership.

Research into pets and human health has revealed a wide range of benefits of pet ownership, including being positively associated with social contact and perceptions of neighbourhood friendliness; lower risk factors for cardiovascular disease; and generally better health than non-pet owners. A study of the relationship between cat ownership and mental health found that cat owners had significantly better scores for psychological health. Pets have been shown to help elderly people whose spouses have died avoid depression, and children with pets have better social skills.

The research proves what people who live with cats already know: our cats give meaning and purpose to our lives; patting them helps us to relax; playing with them makes us laugh and hearing our cats purr makes us smile. When we are lonely they are there for us and when we don't feel well, they comfort us. They never judge us by our looks, our status or our abilities but simply by our kindness. They make us more empathetic because we have to work hard to try to understand them and learn to read subtle visual cues. This in turn makes us better communicators with other people.

Most people now live in cities and are largely disconnected from the natural world that is vital to our wellbeing. While many a farmer will still employ one or several barn cats, most of us no longer need cats to keep the mice away. What our domestic cats do for us now — and possibly what they have always done — is to help us be happier and so healthier, and more compassionate. They provide a bridge to the natural world that reminds us of our place in the universe, of how remarkable life is, and how much we don't know.

Cats have been the subject of many great creative works, and indeed the companions of many great creative people. Jean Cocteau expressed the human–feline bond in saying: 'I love my cats because I enjoy my home, and little by little, they become its visible soul.'

But in six short words, Leonardo da Vinci said it all: 'The smallest feline is a masterpiece.'

ABOUT CATS

Gil Appleton

It's interesting that a name often used for cats — most famously, the early cartoon cat — is Felix, a Latin word generally translated as 'lucky, fortunate, happy'. After all, who is more skilled at looking after Number One, of making sure that they live sybaritic lives of comfort and ease, than domestic cats?

It's virtually impossible to generalise about cats because they are highly individual. Some claim that particular breeds have particular characteristics. The only purebred I have had, Fred — a superb Abyssinian — was certainly a singular cat, whose disconcerting devotion to me bordered on obsession. But having otherwise always had 'moggies' I cannot assess claims of breed-specific characteristics. I will, however, rather boldly attempt to make some observations with which the reader is at liberty to disagree.

My husband Jim McClelland was a late convert to cats, having previously been a dog person. While he still liked dogs, he found cats more interesting because they were so unpredictable. He felt you had to work at making a cat accept you, whereas most dogs are pathetically eager to be liked. Like many converts, Jim became a fanatical cat lover (and patron of the Cat Protection Society), and could be seen every night greeting the cats along our street as he returned from work. The cause of his conversion was Grace, a predominantly white cat with black patches. I had rescued Grace from a pet shop in Grace Brothers where she remained unsold on Christmas Eve. Cats seem to understand and be grateful when they've been rescued from a sad fate, and Grace was devoted, affectionate — and long-suffering. In middle age she had to adapt to a regular 100-kilometre weekend car trip, and in the process devised ever more cunning ways of hiding from us when she sensed a trip was imminent. We in turn resorted to subterfuges such as driving off to convince her that we'd left.

Unlike dogs, who smile a lot and don't take themselves too seriously, cats have no sense of humour. Grace once fell into a fishpond and emerged looking like an old grey dishcloth. She was much offended when we laughed, retreating under a bed and sulking for many hours. Cats can act quite crazy, though, with hilarious results. Every cat I've known has had bursts of sudden, inexplicable dashing through the house, leaping over furniture, climbing curtains, skilfully avoiding (for the most part) valuable items, and just as suddenly calming down and taking up their customary recumbent position.

Cats that look a bit funny — the kind with blotches on their face that have a clownish effect, for example, or those with fur of a particularly strange and not very attractive colour, or who have lost an ear or a limb — are usually the nicest cats of all. They seem to feel they have to work hard to make up for the shortcomings of their appearance.

Contrary to myth, cats are not aloof, but enjoy company. Grace was inclined to jump on the laps of visitors, in one case landing in the lap of Nobel Prize-winning author Patrick White (luckily he loved animals, probably more than people). Unfortunately, most cats have a habit of attaching themselves to the one person in the room who professes to hate them, or has an allergy to them — a rather touching form of attempted conversion.

Cats are fastidious — all right, just plain fussy. Anyone who thinks that all cats like fish and milk has never owned one. I've had cats that wouldn't touch fish or milk. Solo cats feel they have the right to reject any food, probably including Beluga caviar, if they feel so inclined. One possible solution is to have more than one cat, so that meals become a competition. But this backfired in my household when large tabby male Harry, after gobbling his own food, would move swiftly on to that of his companion, dainty Siamese-cross Sally. This led to mealtime separation arrangements of extreme complexity.

Many cats develop strange habits. Harry, when young, would spend hours staring at the floor drain in the bathroom, waiting for the next bath or shower so that he could watch and listen as the water ran away. He grew out of this practice, probably realising at last (he was a bear of very modest brain) that one or two water events a day did not justify the hours he devoted to it. His whip-smart companion Sally, however, once used the bathroom to great effect, jumping into the sink and, most uncharacteristically, peeing into it. To my dismay, I saw that there was blood in her urine. Perhaps she wouldn't have used this method of letting me know had she realised a visit to the vet would ensue. Getting her into a carrier and driving to the vet was an experience requiring the wiles of Machiavelli and nerves of steel.

Cats are tough and resourceful. Many are the tales of cats accidentally shut in empty houses for weeks, or travelling thousands of kilometres to previous homes, surviving on their wits. On my travels I have seen the cats of Rome (an estimated 300,000 of them) living in the ancient monuments and being cared for by an army of locals supported by international donations; the cats of Istanbul, a city where cats are integral and ubiquitous, fed and watered by residents; cats living in a convent near Mount Sinai in Egypt, cared for by the monks. All over the world cats manage to survive.

Closer to home, my current cat, black and white Jessie, in a demonstration of cats' uncanny sense of timing and their ability to find a new human companion, arrived at the door shortly after Harry had died. She was chipped and proved to belong to people several kilometres away. Returned to this home, she was back within a fortnight, travelling through bush and across busy roads. The people relinquished her, saying that she had obviously made her choice. Unfortunately, she had learned to live on her wits, which involved killing and eating native wildlife, and she is now confined to the house and a roomy garden enclosure.

Cats used to a regular routine and surroundings object to the smallest change, such as shifting a piece of furniture, and for these cats moving house is the ultimate terror. However, a friend who restores and sells houses for a living has moved her cat 23 times with the result that this cat adapts calmly to any circumstances, positively leaps into her carrier, and travels quietly for any distance. I've met cats travelling with Grey Nomads who live happily on the road and enjoy meeting new people in every camp site.

It is no wonder we love these complex, fascinating, sensuous, exceptional and beautiful creatures.

THE LOVE FOR THREE CATS

Judy Goyen

This is a story about three Siamese cats: Henry, Daisy and Coco. Henry and Daisy came to live with me when they were both seven years old. Their previous owners had advertised them in the local newspaper as 'free to a good home'. If you had known Henry and Daisy you would have found it very difficult to understand how anyone could have given away such adorable cats but that's another story. What about Coco, I hear you ask? Well she wasn't born at this point in the story so you'll just have to be patient.

When Henry and Daisy first came to live with me they were very frightened and spent the next three or four days hiding under the lounge. Ever so gradually their confidence picked up and in due course they settled in. However they remained fearful of strangers for quite some time.

The two cats had been together all their lives and were very attached to each other, which is why their previous owners had insisted that they not be separated. Daisy was the leader. If she moved into another room, Henry followed. If she changed beds, Henry did too. However Henry was emotionally insecure. He cried if you left him, he cried when you returned and he cried when you ignored him. Daisy on the other hand was much more independent and couldn't understand her brother's immaturity.

When they were about ten years old I moved to a cat-friendly house with more sunlight and a secure garden (they had been indoor cats until then). Unlike their previous relocation, they settled in immediately. They soon learned to use the cat door to venture into their new garden but they never attempted to scale the wall to escape. Life was easy.

But nothing in life stays the same, and about a year after moving, Daisy suffered renal failure and had to be euthanased. I often thought about getting another cat but decided against it because I had heard of cats not getting on with the newcomer. And it was not apparent to me that Henry missed her. He had been demanding before and he was demanding now. Anyhow, I had by now retired and was at home most days to keep him company.

But as I said, nothing in life remains the same and about two years later, Kristina from the Cat Protection Society casually mentioned that they had a female Siamese cat in need of a good home. And this is where Coco enters the story. Coco was a gorgeous six-year-old Seal Point, the same as Daisy, who had been relinquished when her owners went overseas. It was love at first sight and thankfully I was allowed to adopt her. Kristina assured me that the two cats would bond if I introduced them to each other gradually, and this is exactly what I did.

My house has a louvre door that divides the front of the house from the back. I kept Coco in the front half while Henry had to settle for the back. They could see each other through the louvres but could not interact. This arrangement worked well during the day but could not be continued at night as Henry had become accustomed to sleeping with me in the front part of the house and I did not want to discontinue this practice in case he felt rejected. So Coco had to be locked in the guests' bedroom at night while Henry stayed with me. But I didn't want Coco to feel rejected either, so in the small hours of the morning, I would leave Henry and slip into the guests' room to sleep with Coco. This went on for ten days, as Coco developed a cold and had to be kept away from Henry a bit longer than expected. By this stage, Coco was desperate to meet Henry so I opened the louvre door.

They sniffed each other and then promptly ignored each other. What an anti-climax. No problem whatsoever. Later that day, Henry was sleeping in his favourite bed when Coco decided to join him. He moved over, they cuddled up together, and they've been sleeping together ever since. I thought it was a pretty tight fit, so I brought out the old double cat bed that Henry and Daisy used to sleep in, but they have no interest in it. They much prefer to squash up together in a single bed. There are three such beds scattered throughout the house, and you will always find them together in one of them. When Coco moves, Henry follows. He has found himself a new leader.

And what a difference Coco has made to Henry. He has a new lease of life as Coco insists on playing chasings with him at least once a day. He has also developed a hearty appetite and has put on a kilogram in weight.

But that's not all. The most miraculous thing of all is that Henry is no longer the anxious, demanding cat that he once was. Privately, I used to describe

Coco and Henry

him as Henry Paine but now I think of him as Henry Placido. He's not afraid of strangers and he's not afraid of being left on his own. He is just one big happy contented cat. A human would have to spend years in psychotherapy to achieve the same outcome.

And Coco? She delights everyone who meets her. She purrs like a steam engine, is as mischievous as a kitten and warms everyone's heart. Thank you Cat Protection Society for transforming our lives.

INSPIRATION

Danielle Lyonne, Animax Photography

I photograph animals for a living, all animals ... dogs, cats, horses, reptiles, birds, even fish. Some of the animals have included crocodiles, llamas and even a bird-eating spider. All of my work is done with behavioural knowledge of the species/breed, various tricks and noises, heaps of delicious food and treats and, most of all, lots of patience. Well, this goes for all animals except for cats: domestic cats do not think they are little humans, they think we are big cats and treat us accordingly.

My first real cat photography session was a big lesson for me. My first dozen clients all had dogs — easy, a ball, treat or silly noise and job done. Then along came Mishka and Bella (a sweet grey domestic short hair and a very naughty tortie). I walked in the door to overwhelming love and affection from Mishka and a frigid judgmental stare from Bella as she sized me up and decided I didn't come up to her standards, promptly disappearing into the lounge and refusing to come out again until I had left. I walked away with my ego seriously bruised. I've never been the type of person to let a challenge go, so after much internet research on cat psychology we decided to try again with a different approach the following week. This time I entered with all my equipment and proceeded to ignore Bella while having a cup of tea. Eventually curiosity got the better of her and she couldn't resist coming to investigate all the equipment and bags, then she came over to me and we came to an understanding: if I would let her dictate the pace and tempo of the session she would hang around and tolerate me. After this we had a fabulous time and she became quite the little diva — even pouncing on the camera lens when I was trying to entice and capture her brother lounging in a patch of sunshine.

With cats there can be no expectation, only hope and possibility. 'Expect the unexpected and be prepared for anything' is now my mantra when shooting the feline variety. There is nothing better than having that special moment when it all just comes together; when you get the light just right, for example, and capture the amazing detail that is peculiar to a cat's eye, it can look like gold foil in some or bronze or green iridescent flecks in others.

Cats have their own world, their own routines that so often we are quite oblivious to. They choose to let us into their life rather than let us plan theirs. I find it hard to resist the challenge of trying to uncover and show through pictures their private lives.

I love the range of emotion that you can only get from cats: one minute it is all love and smoochy rolls on the floor and then the next they become attack cat when they spot that rogue ping pong ball or feather. From innocence to hunter in under a minute is amazing and when you capture that on film there is no better feeling.

There is a languid beauty to a cat, when they lounge around basking in the sun looking all sleepy and lazy while still giving off the impression that a predator lies beneath. The feats of acrobatics a cat can display are truly mesmerising — the range of movement, the power of their muscles, the height they can jump all while executing a half pike double twist and still managing to land on their feet is impressive.

A unique thing I find when photographing a cat is how my interest in them is reciprocated. I'm watching them trying to work out what they'll do next and they'll be watching me to see what I'll do next, which toys I have brought or which camera or lens needs inspecting. They are as fascinated by something new (me) as I am (them) .

Photo by Danielle Lyonne

I have read that the print on a cat's nose is like that of a human fingerprint, unique. No matter the size, shape or colour, inside them all truly beats the heart of a tiger. I have seen this in every cat I have met and had the privilege to photograph. Some are funny, aloof, enchanting or even outright odd but they are all related to each other by their uniqueness.

A BRIEF CAT ENCOUNTER

Susie Willis

One evening a small black cat strolled up to our back door and asked to be allowed in. She was a friendly little thing. We hadn't seen her in the neighbourhood before, so we were concerned she might be lost. There was a tiny silver canister attached to her collar, which contained a rolled up scroll with her name, Snowball, and a mobile number.

As it was late we texted the mobile with the message, 'Snowball is visiting us in Balmain and we're worried she might be lost'. The owner replied immediately that she had just moved to the area, and in fact lived a couple of doors from us in our rear laneway, so we wandered out and met Snowball's pyjama-wearing owner. It turned out she had three cats, tiny black Snowball and two larger grey cats, one named Sampson. The three were littermates.

The next evening Snowball came back with her friends. We thought it best not to encourage them, so didn't allow them inside. When we went to bed we could hear them rustling outside our bedroom window — they were very persistent, so eventually we opened the window and they came in and plonked themselves on the bed.

Over the next few weeks we became very well acquainted with all three cats. There began a ritual of us leaving the window slightly open each evening and sleeping every night with one to three cats on our bed. It was a delightful experience. They were the friendliest and most beautifully mannered cats.

Around that time my husband and I got the flu, so for maybe a week there was always someone in bed during the day. The cats took full advantage of this situation and stayed all day as well as the nights. It must have been heaven for a cat: a huge, comfy bed with someone prepared to cuddle and stroke them 24 hours a day.

We were very sad when we learned the owner was planning to move to Tasmania. They'd only been residents for maybe a month. My husband and I discussed whether we might ask the owner if we could keep Sampson (of whom we'd become particularly fond) in exchange for an extremely generous amount of money. We also talked about the idea of locking Sampson in our house until the owner had moved! After all, she had three cats; surely she wouldn't miss one ...

Sadly (and rightly) all three cats left for Tasmania. We still miss them.

PEPPER AND COTTON SOCKS

Nicky Barraclough

We adopted Pepper in 2008, after fostering her for about two-and-a-half months. I had just started my new job working at Cat Protection and was told that the best way to get to know cats was to foster them. I had no idea at the time how much this one little cat would change our lives.

It was a busy start to the kitten season in October 2008 when we had run out of foster carers. Late one afternoon some distressed people rushed a scrawny and very angry mother cat into us; someone in their neighbourhood had moved out and locked her in the empty house with no food or water, left by herself to give birth alone.

After a few days of her being locked in the house the neighbours rallied together and broke a window to get her out. When they got to her she was lying down with four tiny little babies, two ginger and two black and white. As they put the box down on the counter I peered in at this very terrified and *very* angry mother cat, doing only what she knew, protecting her babies from the humans who had betrayed her in the past.

As we'd run out of foster carers I was asked if I would take her on, so I said yes. I had never been so scared of a cat — as I sat in the office waiting for her to be put in a cat carrier I could hear her screaming with anger and lunging towards the cage, doing anything she could to keep her babies safe.

As my partner picked me up from work that afternoon I handed him the carry cage. The whole cage rumbled with growls and hisses. I think he was as scared as I was. All I could think to myself was, 'I can't believe I'm bringing a feral cat into my home!' We got her home and set up our bathroom for her, laying down towels on the floor and making a nest for her. It came time to let her out and get the kittens out too. I put the cage in the bathroom, opened the door and stood back as if it were a tiger I had just released. Out came this little cat, ears back, tail down, walking as low to the ground as possible. She was emotionally broken, you could just see it in her eyes. I put her kittens in her nest for her and she did all the rest!

Day by day she got better and better, eventually moving her kittens into our bedroom to sleep near us. The hardest adjustment was getting used to an animal who had no trust for me, let alone my 6-foot tall partner; it took her months to get used to him (she saw him as a giant in the house). The kittens were about five weeks old, and we were learning week by week everything and anything there was to know about cats and kittens — it was great! But no one could have prepared us for her being on heat. I had never heard such loud cries! Every night for about a week.

It came to the end of our time fostering this little cat whom we had named Pepper. In the days leading up to bringing her back for adoption, my partner and I just looked at her, not knowing what to do. We were heartbroken. We decided to adopt her in the end, as she had so much trouble building up trust we couldn't bear to betray her trust again. It has now been almost three years since we adopted Pepper and we have never regretted it. It took four months before she would leave our bedroom for the first time and about eight months to stop running away from my partner. We couldn't be happier. She sleeps in the bed every night with us, gets excited when she knows we're home and loves it when we have people over. She sits in the middle of our coffee table and rolls around expecting all guests to give her scratches (even if they don't like cats). She went from weighing about 3 kilograms and being horribly underweight to now weighing a healthy 7½ kilograms.

All her kittens found loving and responsible homes and some of their owners still send us photos to this day. After this, my partner now has very strong views on responsible cat ownership and desexing (something I never thought he would have an interest in). Pepper has even rubbed off on my brother who now loves giving her treats, scratches and head butts. If you had told me we were going to adopt her on that first day we took her home I never would have believed you, but now she has just blossomed into the perfect cat. People always ask me how I got her and they never believe me when I tell them what she was like. She is an inspiration to me. If she can get through that and trust again, we can get through anything!

Pepper

In October 2010 another special cat came into my life when Cotton Socks was handed in to the Cat Protection shelter in Newtown. She was underweight, riddled with fleas and had one very badly damaged eye. Poor little thing, we thought, she was only about ten or twelve weeks old and already life had dealt her some serious challenges.

She got her name from the little girl who had looked after her until Cat Protection was able to take her; the little girl was in love with her but already had a number of cats. Cotton's fate was now in Cat Protection's hands. The decision was made to save her little life and carry out an operation to remove the damaged eye, and to see whether there was treatment available to stop the remaining eye from deteriorating further.

Cotton came back from the vet after her operation with a face full of stiches, but she still purred and cuddled as if nothing had ever happened. It was too soon after an operation like that to re-home her so we decided to put her into foster care. Fate intervened next.

My mother had been a foster parent for Cat Protection for about two years; she had lots of experience with kittens of all shapes, sizes and disabilities. Her first ever foster kitten had also had surgery to remove an eye, so we thought she would be perfect for Cotton Socks. I called her while she was at work and put it to her: 'Mum this is a very special one!' I said. She replied, 'Call your father and ask him,' so I did. My father can see my work number calling on his phone, so after so many foster kittens he now sees my number and answers the phone with 'How many? And When?' In this case I said 'one' and that was it!

That night I took Cotton to my mother's house and put her in her little bed. She was shaking, scared of the new place, the new smells and also Roxy, my mum's big fluffy Ragdoll (also from Cat Protection) who *loves* foster kittens. Roxy ran up to her, licked her, then licked the stitched up eye. We had to put a plastic cone on Cotton's head — not to stop her picking at her stiches but to stop Roxy the Ragdoll licking them out.

A week went by and she went back to the vet for a check-up. There were concerns over her remaining eye, so we tried some new medications. Mum had bonded with Cotton and was happy to care for this little kitten for as long as it took. Weeks went by and still my mother was caring for her.

My mum started to worry about Cotton's welfare and whether she would be able to come back to the shelter. After looking after Cotton for almost three months, we were at our final vet appointment. The vet told us that putting her into the adoption centre would do her more harm than good as her eyesight could get worse, and she also couldn't guarantee what would happen in the future; she could be fine and keep her sight or get worse. When I told Mum she started crying. We spent two days with tears all around, trying to decide the fate of Cotton. We spoke to the vet again and she told us that Cotton could live a happy, healthy, normal life with my mother because she had already made a mental map of her house (which she would need if her eyesight worsened) but that re-homing her to a new house was the issue; too much strain on her little brain.

It was decided. Mum was going to adopt Cotton. I think we secretly knew from the first vet appointment, though, that this was going to happen. One year on, Cotton now lives a happy, healthy life. There have been no further problems with her and her eyesight has improved. My mum and Cotton are the purr-fect match. They are just smitten with each other. Cotton has also made a lifelong connection with Roxy the Ragdoll; they sleep together (curled up like yin and yang), eat together and play together. My mum couldn't imagine her life without Cotton now. Cats really do pick their owners.

RILEY

Nash

I would like to share my story about my best friend, Riley.

Riley is a three-year-old golden puddy tat with lovely long elegant legs and beautiful big green eyes who joined my family from the Cat Protection Society in 2008.

From day one Riley fitted into my life with absolute ease and pleasure. He's adorable, lovable and *so* playful (even years on) and he helps me run the household.

Riley's absolute favourite game is soccer-dice, where he brings the dice to Daddy (me) who throws it down the hall (floorboards) and Riley darts after it and flicks it about, dribbling the dice around until it stops rolling. Then he picks it up, brings it back to Daddy and flicks it out of his mouth onto the floor, which means 'again, again'. This can go on and on and on ... until he gets puffed, of course. Another fun game we play is the brush and walk, our grooming game. Riley doesn't like standing or sitting still when I brush him. He likes to wander around very slowly while I follow him and brush him. If I stop, he turns and meows until I start again.

Over the years Riley has become a more inquisitive cat and won't settle until he has explored every inch of our home — even to the point of jumping on top of cupboards only to have everything fall down after

Riley

him ... never on top of him, he's too quick. He also loves sitting in my room next to the window, watching the cars go by down on the street. He just can't get enough of those strange noisy things that just keep coming and coming and coming.

One way I know when I'm in Riley's good books is when he gives me a good stare and then a long slow squint. As he is a very vocal cat (you can have conversations with him, and it's better than watching television after work) you always know he's around and when he needs something (like a brush or a little treat).

I've taught Riley a few things over the years, such as how to shake hands when he was a little kitten — he now sits there and holds out his little paw for you to hold and shake. He's such a dude. Back in the day of teaching Riley the difference between right and wrong, I employed the idea of using a water pistol. This turned out to be a new game ... be naughty, listen for Daddy, then *hide!* It did not matter how hard I tried to get him with the water pistol, he always fled the scene of the crime. Needless to say, the terrible teens are behind us now.

One major lesson Riley has taught me is that the best way to a happy household is with lots of love. The more love I give, the more he returns. Riley is at his happiest when I am at my happiest. He'll run to the door when I get home from work and yell hello, follow me into my room when it's bed time, sleep on my chest, knead my belly (to make it comfy), head butt me whenever I get on the floor with him, cuddle me when I'm watching television, follow me around and chat when he's in the mood, and he loves to be on my shoulder while I walk around the house. He's my little buddy.

I could go on and on about Riley. He is the most adorable puddy tat and I love him very much. From the day he joined our home it was clear that Riley and Daddy had a special bond, one that will last forever.

Yours with purrs and cuddles,

Nash and Riley

FOSTERING KITTENS

Polly Rickard

Since childhood I've always had cats and when I first thought of fostering kittens I put off the decision because I was sure I wouldn't want to part with them when the time came for them to be permanently adopted. Then one day in 2008, my granddaughter and I were walking past Cat Protection and she told me that it was time to at least go in and put my name down. Thank you, Matilda. That was the beginning of a wonderful adventure.

In no time at all we had our first foster kittens. They were with us for four weeks and everyone fell in love with them. I kept notes of their weight, development and individual traits, as well as taking hundreds of photographs to give them a back story to take with them to their forever homes. One day I made a little polar fleece teddy bear with a bell in it which they seemed to like, and that was the beginning of sending every kitten off to their new home with a biography, a CD of photographs and a teddy bear.

Since then there have been other litters of various ages; some stayed for only two weeks, others for two months, but all of them were hard to let go of. Little Cat X, Little Cat Z, Tallulah, Josephine, Spats, Jet, Smudge, Baby Rose, Leon, Dashi, Spike, Charlie, Pippi, Jasper, Minky, Lulu, Rupert — all perfect.

One litter of four was only two weeks old when they arrived and had to be bottle fed every four hours day and night for the following two weeks. I was enchanted by the way they held the bottle in their little paws, and that enchantment got me through the late night and early morning feeds. Then came weaning, which went quite well except for the kitten I called Baby Rose. She refused to give up her bottle for a full ten days after the others had started to eat and lap. I had visions of bottle feeding a fully grown cat, but eventually she decided to grow up and got to the magic 1 kilogram. They always seem to get to the magic 1 kilo weight too soon and taking them back to Cat Protection is always hard.

I felt very lucky to have had such young kittens and thought it couldn't get any better. Then, in October 2008 I was asked if I'd foster a mother and kittens. When I asked how many kittens I was told that she hadn't yet given birth. How exciting! When Cleo arrived (before she got her name) she was very young, very pregnant, very neglected and very scared. Everyone thought she'd give birth immediately but she waited ten days, during which time I slept with her in case she needed help. She didn't. At midnight on 19 October I woke to find one kitten and was able to video the birth of the other three. Of course, Cleo didn't have them in the nest I'd prepared but behind a large box on a blanket put down to stop draughts coming under the door. Amazingly, she allowed me to transfer her kittens to the large, comfortable, warm and dark cupboard where they stayed for several days. Cleo also adopted an abandoned three-day-old kitten that Sam from the Cat Protection Society brought round the morning after to see whether Cleo would feed him. She immediately adopted him. One week later Sam arrived with a day-old kitten who was also taken into the fold. I was amazed at the way she handled the different ages and sizes, which surely must have been confusing for a cat not much more than a kitten herself. Cleo turned out to be a wonderful mother who was still feeding the six kittens after they were eating solid food. In fact, she was still feeding them when they went back to Cat Protection to go to their forever homes.

It was so hard to let them go, but because we'd had them since birth I was able to take over a thousand photographs of every phase of their lives, although having so many photos to choose from made it very difficult to know which to put on their CDs. I was privileged to watch them learn to walk, then play, then climb, then destroy the lounge chairs — which had been prepared earlier by previous litters.

One of Polly's fosters

We decided to keep Cleo because she was so shy and needy — and not very pretty. She was a strange shape because of starvation and her coat was very patchy and thin. She's been with us for two years now and has grown into a very pretty cat with a most wonderful temperament. Cleo is still obsessed with food and probably always will be, but we can live with that. I'm always amazed at how quickly a starving stray who will eat anything at all becomes a gourmet and will only eat meat from a certain butcher. But that's okay because we love her.

Fostering is a wonderful way to volunteer. Each kitten is different and special and has their own charm and personality. Watching their individual progress from stage to stage is fascinating, and there's nothing better than seeing kittens chase each other through a tunnel or plot to steal a fluffy toy. Fostering involves a lot of work, lack of sleep and curtailing of plans, not to mention the tears when you take them back. But ultimately it's a lot of fun.

GENTLEMAN TOBY

Barb Slifer

I first met Toby one day while I was volunteering at the Cat Protection Society, and a lovely old gentleman he was. At nineteen years old he was still a beautiful ginger cat who carried his age well.

Toby's story is sad but at the same time heart-warming. A few years before, Toby's owner, an elderly gentleman who explained he had been diagnosed with terminal cancer, brought his companion of many years into the CPS and asked them to look after him. Too old to be adopted, and not happy being with other cats, Toby became a bit of a mascot around the Cat Protection Society. He lived in the office area, sunned himself on their balcony and was taken home by various members of the staff.

Toby was a very easy cat to love. When he came home with me he was affectionate and followed me everywhere. He looked so cute when he slept as he always slept with his paw over his nose. He enjoyed sunning himself on my balcony and he never put a paw wrong. It made me realise how satisfying it must be to adopt an older cat, rather than kittens, who need so much training and attention.

Toby lived to the ripe old age of twenty, cared for and loved thanks to the compassion of the wonderful people at the Cat Protection Society.

TEACHING THE LANGUAGE OF CATS

Kate Holland

Originally our human male was allergic to us. He told our human female that he could not be around cats *at all*. Our human female said she understood but then sent special signals out to various members of our species asking for our help.

We had various emissaries approach the male with promises of great joy but none of their calls was quite getting through.

One day human male and human female bought a brand new townhouse in which no human had ever resided. One of ours lived in the area and she heard that 'special call'. Human male could not resist her soft meow while he waited for the movers to arrive with their furniture. He looked at her eyes and she gave a deep welcoming purr. Human male decided the poor thing was starving, little knowing she had just polished off some chicken next door. He opened the tin of salmon the human female had brought for their lunch and said, 'We can have cucumber and cream cheese. This poor thing is starving.' Human female admonished him not because of the salmon but because he said that he was highly allergic to cats and his eyes were already red and he needed a tissue, badly. But our leader had broken through his pain barrier and wrapped herself around his ankles.

Our special agent visited a few more times, staying longer in the house each time. Yes, the male's eyes still ran and he needed lots of tissues but that did not seem to matter. He loved to hear her trill when he came home as she guided him to the kitchen.

They decided to name the agent Flic, and boy did she live up to that name. Rats were her specialty and the humans soon learned the special sound of her call when she had her mouth full. They also learned to look out the window before they let her in the house. This became a necessity when early one morning the female opened the door to let Flic out, and while the human's back was turned Flic came back in and ran up the stairs with that special call. Unfortunately the male was asleep and only realised Flic was there when she dropped a very dead rat on his chest. Flic was very light on her feet, even with a mouth full of dead rat.

Human male was won over and was fascinated by the various calls of Flic. She had friends she invited over on a regular basis to play and between her call and her playmates' answers the human male learned the language of cat.

Flic was desexed and a very social cat. She would meow a few times and if the clumsy cat across the road was out he would come to play among the plants and also be in awe of her climbing abilities. When the same cat became stuck up a tree Flic's demanding and constant meow continued until the human male followed her outside to see what the problem was. A neighbourhood effort was necessary to get Mr Clumsy out of the tree.

Human male was completely cured of his allergy and has now been the caretaker of a number of our tribe. He is fluent in cat-speak and loves nothing better than to have a conversation with our species, so long as the rugby is not on television. He loves us and realises now that life is not complete unless you have cat hair on your clothes.

He still does not open the door without looking at the current cat's mouth, though.

Over the past twenty years we have been fortunate in having five cats, of whom Flic was one, and all of them were adopted by us as adult cats. Too often it seems these cats are overlooked in favour of a kitten and while it is hard to resist a kitten and their 'attitude', most adult cats still have a lot of kitten left in them; you just need to find it. More importantly, the adult cat still has a ton of love to share.

It has been a conscious decision of ours to adopt adult cats simply because both of us work and a kitten initially needs a lot more human contact than an adult cat does. We have never regretted these decisions and the amount of love we have received from our cats cannot be measured.

This is not to say, however, that there are no drawbacks in either selection. With an adult cat adoption you do not have the full history of the cat's personality so therefore you must select carefully if you have small children. Some cats have not been around children or have been inadvertently injured by them and the cat will not be comfortable and therefore may strike out. Also, with an adult cat you might have one who has never been around stairs or balconies and these, of course, can be a challenge. In some cases adult cats that have been surrendered can be very timid and require quite a bit of coaxing and careful handling in order to help the cat to come out of their shell. Once that has been accomplished you will find the cat is devoted to you. Well, as much as a cat can be devoted to anyone other than themself.

Kittens need to be trained as to what is acceptable and what is not (no, they are not supposed to eat the food off your plate while you are having dinner, no matter how cute they are!). Unless they are contained in a safe area, kittens can get into a lot, and I mean a lot, of trouble without supervision. Electric cords, washing machines, the space behind refrigerators — all these provide loads of interesting fun but are very dangerous. And that is just inside the house. Kittens have not yet learned there is danger outside and will need careful supervision in this area.

Most adult cats enjoy playing as much as kittens do, they just don't play for as long as a kitten does. There are more important things to the adult cat — like food, warm laps and sunshine. We need to encourage our friends and associates to consider adopting an adult cat if they are thinking of acquiring a feline. Too often these cats are surrendered because they are no longer small and have reached an age where they need annual veterinarian care. It is not that expensive but unfortunately there are cases where people just cannot afford it.

Adult cats are very loving, playful and already trained. Very rarely do they try to steal your food (well, almost rarely) but they don't climb the curtains anymore, they know what the litter box is for, and they like to sleep in more. That is a selling point in itself when you work five days a week!

SANDY AND PIGSY

Tara Johnson

Sandy and Pigsy think the world of each other.

From their time as littermates, their adventures together at the Cat Protection Society and finally to their forever home in Newtown and then Queensland, these two chaps have stuck together as only best friends can.

They've been glued together since kittenhood. Wherever Pigsy is sleeping, Sandy wants to be there, too. When Sandy finds a prime snoozing spot, Pigsy is right there beside him. No matter how small the space or impossible the obstacles, these two always find their way to each other and unite in a comfortable-looking ball of heads and paws and tails. They wouldn't have it any other way.

When they're not snoozing, Sandy and Pigsy spend their days running up and down the house, chasing each other and generally acting like loons. Their antics naturally progress into wrestling and play-fighting, but never at the expense of brotherly affection. Once the battles are over, they'll find a cosy nook to settle down in and give each other long, loving baths.

Sandy, the smaller of the two, loves sleeping upside-down like a baby, sitting on laps and frequent nuzzles. Though sometimes shy, he is never above meowing loudly and triumphantly to announce his wish for

Sandy and Pigsy

affection, supper or play. Pigsy is a huge foodie. Rumour has it he has made off with more than one loaf of bread and once an entire steak — but he'd deny it. He's much too busy relieving Sandy of his supper, then making up for it by giving him generous baths.

Sandy and Pigsy now live in Queensland. They can't say they enjoyed the trip up much, but now that they're here they've embraced the lifestyle. They're usually found catching the Queensland breeze out on the deck or showing off their stylish new haircuts. Life is good, and apart from a brief period of estrangement when Sandy disappeared to have surgery, these two adventurers are doing just fine.

Brothers, wrestlers and snooze-mates, Sandy and Pigsy are the best of friends.

MARY, MARY, SMALL AND WARY

Judith McCreath

Who knows where Mary appeared from? Any time of day or night, on the busy suburban street Mary might be seen dodging traffic, on her way to where? Was she searching for someone or for food, for a cuddle or a bed? By day, a small fluffy tortoiseshell cat with a snow leopard's tail flashed by, and by night — was that that little cat?

This cat appeared on our patio one evening, I guessed she was homeless. Each evening, for some months, she would sit there and I would go outside with cat biscuits and place a little bowl down, and each evening Mary would express her gratitude by hissing. One evening I placed the bowl down and when she hissed I had my say: I requested that she stop being so absolutely ridiculous, and she did. Mary never hissed at me again and we became friends.

Mary must have been someone's cat at some stage because she wanted a cuddle every evening before she ate. I wondered if an elderly person had gone to a nursing home, or perhaps had even died, leaving Mary with no place to be? Even worse, I imagined that perhaps she had been a 'pet', one who had been left behind when someone moved. 'Where's the cat?' 'Oh don't worry, cats can fend for themselves — it'll be all right, it won't settle anywhere else anyway. It'll manage, they always fall on their feet. Come on, hurry up ...' I fear this is the most likely explanation. Why does this happen? How can we humans do this? Was Mary disposable, like a broken plastic toy? Was this sentient, sensible, sensitive little being something to be dumped, like rubbish left over from a garage sale, before a move?

Mary adopted me and it was she who told me her name was Mary, I think. One evening as she sat on the patio the name Mary came into my head. I tried it out and she answered to her name, or maybe it was just my voice she responded to, but Mary she was. Mary was a very attractive cat — several tomcats will vouch for this — so, although I originally thought she might have been desexed, once her general health and condition improved and the omens were auspicious several suitors arrived. The toms were something of a nuisance — yowling, fighting and generally disturbing the peace — not so good for my neighbours, who did pass comment more than once. They also posed a threat to Mary's safety and I thank the heavens that no one called the council cat-catcher or Mary would have been taken and put down immediately.

Mary eventually became pregnant. One evening at Easter, after she'd eaten her food, I noticed that she'd gone from having a full tummy of babies in the morning to once again being the tiny little cat she had been before the toms came. It was bucketing down rain that weekend. Between me and my neighbour there is an almost impenetrable thicket of vines and slim-stemmed, woody trees, a no-man's-land, a fortress, which now held a secret. When Mary had eaten she disappeared into this tangled undergrowth and as I searched I found her curled up in a ball trying to keep her newborn babies warm, dry and alive as the run-off of rain coursed all around them. With the help of one kind neighbour, Mary allowed us to take her soaking wet babies into my old, dry garage and place them on a lambskin rug in a small wicker dog basket. Mary just followed me with no protest and there they lived and thrived.

Cat and kitten milk, water, cat biscuits and, later, kitten biscuits and finely chopped poached chicken, strokes, cuddles and gentle voices and

kitty litter were the order of the day, twice a day, for the next seven weeks. By that time the babies had names, had been handled every day and came running as quickly as Mary when they heard both my voice and my granddaughter's. They were beautiful, bold, playful kittens and they had the most devoted and wonderful mother in Mary.

Three of the babies went to one home. They now live with a wonderful, caring family who had lost two beloved cats, both aged twenty, in 2010. The two remaining kittens were accepted by the Cat Protection Society and were adopted within two weeks. The society offered to take Mary too, for desexing and adoption, providing she had no microchip and did not have ringworm; Mary had neither and though she was frightened she allowed the kind young woman at the society to handle her when I took her there, so it was obvious she was not feral. I was unable to offer Mary a permanent home, though I would have done so in an instant if two small animals had been allowed in the place I was moving to. I cried when I left her, but I could never leave her to fend for herself again and to have litter after litter of kittens until her small body could take it no longer and she died of malnutrition, disease and serial birth.

More than likely Mary had never had any veterinary care: no vaccinations, desexing, worming or check-ups. In her pre-op examination it was discovered that she had an extremely enlarged heart and could not survive an operation. She was put to sleep, without fear or pain, in the caring environment of Cat Protection. How she survived so long with this fatal condition, and how she was able to produce kittens, we will never know, but Mary was a special and wonderful girl. She had the heart of a lioness, the strength of a jaguar, the beauty of a tiger and the tail of a snow leopard. She was a loving friend, a wonderful mother and a wonderful cat and I miss and love her. Goodbye little girl Mary, the tiniest 'big cat'. I will never forget you.

HAKUNA MATATA: A WORRY-FREE PHILOSOPHY

Jessica Arciuli

I knew it was love the moment I saw him. He was but a day old and didn't yet resemble a cat. His mother, Lily, was beautiful: black as the night with stunning golden eyes. There were four in the litter, including him. Two girls and two boys, all black and white.

It was December 2008, I was sixteen and I had just lost my beloved ginger cat, Biscuit. He had passed away on Christmas Eve from a rare condition known as feline aortic thromboembolism. It was heartbreaking — he was my first pet and had been given to me by my mum for my eleventh birthday. I had wanted a pet cat all my life, particularly because I am an only child and spent a lot of my time dreaming about having a companion. Biscuit and I were inseparable and I absolutely adored him.

I decided it was too soon to get a new pet straight after Biscuit died, but thought that perhaps taking care of a cat for a little while might help me heal. So I became a foster carer for the Cat Protection Society. Eager to get my hands on my first foster litter, I went to the shelter as soon as I could to volunteer my services. I was introduced to Lily and her four kittens. Instantly her dazzling golden eyes (much like Biscuit's) took me and I accepted responsibility for her and her babies then and there. I was to have them for the next eight weeks, until they were old enough to be homed.

The first few weeks were rather uneventful. Lily was a spectacular mother and needed no assistance with her children aside from the occasional break so she could have her 'me time'. The kittens were sleeping and suckling and not much else. I loved holding them in the palm of my hand and planting little kisses on their foreheads, and Lily was always obliging.

As they grew, they developed real personalities and became quite rambunctious. That is, all but one: Pumba. I had named him after the warthog in the popular children's movie *The Lion King* because of his impressive size and his happy-go-lucky attitude. Pumba played occasionally, to keep his brother and sisters amused, but he was always much happier to observe happenings from the couch. He was a contented little fellow, relaxed and peaceful. He had the most beautiful fur, the softest I had ever felt on a cat, and when I stroked him he melted.

I was taking it in turns sleeping with one kitten on my bed per night, to help them become accustomed to humans and to wean them off their mummy. All the kittens hated being away from their mum and siblings except Pumba. He seemed to love sleeping at the foot of my bed and always purred loudly.

The kittens were eight weeks old before I knew it but I wasn't ready to let go. I asked the lovely people at Cat Protection if I could have one more week with the little rascals and they granted me my wish. I started thinking about how quiet the house would be when they left, how much I had enjoyed their presence, and how it had helped me cope so much with the loss of Biscuit. I knew I loved all the kittens already, but I had really taken a shine to Pumba, and he to me. After much deliberation with my mum (and Lily), I decided I was going to adopt Pumba. I was ecstatic.

Pumba is now two and a half years old and still my baby. He is a huge cat, weighing in at 6 kilograms, and his carefree disposition has blossomed into a full-blown problem-free philosophy — 'hakuna matata'. And he is

a real character. For such a large cat you wouldn't believe the boxes he manages to get himself into. He is obsessed, it seems, with contorting himself into all kinds of positions in order to fit into tiny boxes and baskets. He ends up head at tail, paws in all directions, all tucked up, but looks perfectly comfortable and will stay where he is for hours. When a new box arrives in the house, he feels a need to inspect it and spend at least a few hours deciding if it will become a permanent fixture in the house or just a passing phase. He really gives each box a fair go.

Another one of his eccentricities is his fixation on drinking water from a glass, fresh from the tap. He will run from one side of the house to the other when he hears a tap run. He will then circle your feet with his fluffy tail high in the air, until you fill up a glass and place it on the floor for him to drink, an activity which always results in a large puddle forming on the floor.

Pumba is also an extremely sociable cat. Every time someone comes home he makes a point of greeting them at the door and leading them into the house. By no means is Pumba a lap cat, but he takes great comfort in being in the presence of people. He will often be found in his box in the study when someone is working on the computer or on his favourite chair in the living room when someone is watching television.

Despite his charms, he isn't always so gentlemanly; he can be quite the audacious cat. My grandfather, Serge, is usually the one to feed him his much loved meals, and Pumba knows what time they are fed to him. This, however, does not stop him from pressuring my grandfather prematurely. He will sit at the foot of Serge's favourite couch and stare at him intensely. He will place his paw on the edge of the couch, right next to Serge's leg and will not move until Serge gives in — which he always does eventually.

It certainly has been an amazing journey, one I hope will continue for many years to come. I am nearly twenty years old now and while I have become much more independent and do not dream about companionship as often as I did as an eleven-year-old girl, I cherish my little (not so little) warthog immensely.

TIGER LILLY'S WORLD

Leanne and Chris Pearce

Welcome to Tiger Lilly's world. Tiger Lilly is a small tabby and is the head of our furry entertainment committee. We adopted her a year ago and she has become the furry boss of Sammi (Standard Poodle), Jamila (Greyhound) and Lizzie (Afghan Hound).

When she arrived home Tiger Lilly strutted out of her carry box and proceeded to investigate everything in sight. I must admit that we did have a few troubles introducing her to the other girls but after several weeks of persistent introductions they all got on well.

Never an evening goes past when Jamila isn't racing through the house with Tiger Lilly in hot pursuit — the sight of a Greyhound being chased by a cat isn't one to be missed. One of Tiger Lilly's other pastimes is to wait for Lizzie to lie down then pounce on her long hairy ears; an Afghan Hound's hair is just irresistible to her and she can also be found hanging off her tail hair. Poor Sammi is also harassed by Tiger Lilly, as she pounces on paws, swipes at feet and generally makes Sammi move from her snoozing spot.

The outdoor cat run is one of Tiger Lilly's joys. She can often be found reclining in her hammock gazing ponderously at the birds in the trees beside the run. I'm certain she thinks they are there for her

entertainment. She can come and go into the house as she pleases and there are always favourite places she can be found. She adores tennis balls and her knitted blanket that she drags around the house.

When friends come over with their dogs Tiger Lilly will walk up to them and check them out. Midget, an overzealous puppy, once came to visit and having never seen a cat proceeded to play bow and bark at Tiger Lilly. Tiger Lilly just fluffed herself up and pounced at Midget, sending the puppy running off in any direction away from Tiger Lilly as fast as possible only to find herself being chased. Tiger Lilly has a new playmate.

Tiger Lilly is always plotting how she can get the fish in our big fish tank. There are several large fish that speed around the tank when her furry head pops into view. I'm quite certain that the fish are teasing her but then I'm equally sure Tiger Lilly is sizing them up for an in-between meal snack. Her attempts to catch them have failed, with her sliding off the tank lid and onto the floor. She will then meow and run off to find a dog to annoy.

The only place Tiger Lilly is not allowed is the backyard. We had made the decision that she was to be an indoors-only cat, hence the cat run. She has made several attempts to see the wide outdoors, only to be herded in by Sammi who has made the decision that she isn't supposed to be outside and must be brought in immediately.

CATS AND CHILDREN

Adrienne Jansen-Howard

It was while searching through the Cat Protection Society's website cats for adoption that I came across a pair of big beautiful blue–green eyes that seemed to reflect a wise old soul and a kitten-like playfulness ... I knew that this beautiful girl, Ness, was meant to be our new family member. I was on the phone to my husband in a heartbeat — and then rang the CPS to ensure this beautiful girl was still there.

That weekend we gathered up our cat carrier and headed to the CPS to meet Ness and see whether we were suitable parents — and to see whether or not she wanted to own us, too. Upstairs we went to see her sitting on a big plush pillow like a queen, while other cats and people milled around her. I approached carefully and seemed to get the seal of approval; hubby wasn't so sure, but I was absolutely adamant she was meant to be ours and so home she came.

We took Ness upstairs to our bedroom and en suite (already kitted out with kitty litter, water, food, scratching post, cosy blankets on the bed) and we put her big plush pillow in the wardrobe so she could have that spot too. When we let her out, she became a big kitten — smooching, dribbling, purring and jumping on the bed and pounding away at the blanket. 'What a different cat,' said a happy hubby. I spent the next two

Ness   *Annabelle and Ness*

days just sitting on the bed with her watching television and giving her lots of attention as she got used to all the strange noises from outside. Every day the following week I would shoot home from work at lunchtime to see her — always being greeted with smooching, which was lovely. Over the next few weeks we introduced her to the rest of the house and eventually the backyard; she of course took over the house — and my hubby's attention!

Around six months later, I found out that I was pregnant. All through my pregnancy, Ness always seemed to know when my hormones were going nuts and would come and sit with me, purring and smooching. And she always had hubby wrapped around her little paw.

My beautiful baby girl, Anabelle, arrived in October. Ness was at the boarding cattery for the week while I was in hospital. While there, hubby took a cloth in which we had wrapped Anabelle to the cattery to put in with Ness so she was used to the smell of our new baby. Once home, Ness was always lovely with Bella and never tried to harm her. She used to come and sit with us while Anabelle fed, or she would lie next to Bella under the play gym but she always seemed to be watchful and curious.

These days, Ness has become very tolerant of my now toddler and though Bella has copped a few scratches, on the whole Ness doesn't harm her — in fact they even play peek-a-boo and watch kids' programs together — and, needless to say, Ness has found plenty of comfy sleeping spots amongst Bella's toys.

This year another new addition arrived — another baby girl, Alexandra. Ness again has been lovely; she especially enjoys sleeping on our bed while Alexandra is sound asleep, although disappears in a flash when bub starts yelling!

Ness used to disappear for the entire day (upstairs to our room or the cupboard) whenever children were around, but nowadays she's content to hang around and see if she can get some attention — or food! She is quick to disappear, however, if toys come flying her way or little hands start flapping at her, but most of the time she just sits and watches all the action.

Adopting Ness (or should I say Ness adopting us) was one of the best things that happened to our family. We adore her and we know that as our daughters grow up she will become treasured by them just as much as she is by us.

MILO AND ME

Sarah Eves

When I went to the CPS seven years ago I never imagined that I would be leaving with the Ginger Beast! However, once he chose me I did not stand a chance.

I can remember the day clearly. When I walked into the room, Milo came to the cage door and started 'talking' to me. I was not there looking for a cat for myself; rather, I was accompanying a friend. Being a sucker for kittens I played with some, but kept coming back to Milo. The attendant offered to get him out for me and I thought, if nothing else, he'd get a cuddle. He snuggled into my arms, chirped away to me and cemented his place in my life at that moment.

When I returned to collect Milo I was told that it was supposed to be. He was apparently an aloof cat who'd been at the shelter for some time without anyone showing much interest in him, and he had not responded to anyone as he had to me.

There is a lot of truth in people being the servants of cats — especially in this house! Milo likes to get what he wants, when he wants, and knows all the tricks in the book to guarantee my attention, including banging blinds, pushing things off the bedside table, pawing the lamp and talking away, earning himself the nickname Squeaky. Milo has been a good teacher to my two Great Danes — ensuring that they know he rules the house, and teaching them how to be gentle while he endures the inquisitive puppy stage as they clean his ears and leave slobber on him. In return he likes nothing more than to smooch their muzzles and tickle their stomachs with his tail.

In choosing me that day, Milo certainly changed my life and I'll always be grateful to the CPS for this.

ANGEL BREATH

Jean V. Leyendekkers

The ground where I stand used to be our vegetable patch. Now it is too shady to grow vegetables so we buy them. Keira, our part-Persian calico is snooping around here. What the heck is she after? Then I hear it: a sort of high-pitched bird sound and Kiera has found the creature, a tiny fragment of catness, a black kitten so small she almost fits in my hand. So velvety soft with a little nick in the tail and, how charming, a white heart-shaped area on her chest. She is so soft and sweet I feel she is female and, yes, she is as I pick her up and look. Her eyes peer up, bluish, so young. I take her down to the house, Keira padding behind. I put her in a cardboard box filled with towels. Kurt falls in love at first look. We think of how to feed her. I ring up the vet. 'She is so young she can't lap,' I explain. 'I have a doll's feeder bottle, yes.' He tells me of a suitable formula; I make it up and rush to the kitten to give it to her. The little creature grabs the bottle in her paws and sucks and sucks, her little ears flapping madly like an elephant's, and when the bottle is drained she whacks it angrily.

Later in the evening I make up some sandy stuff in a tray and set it near her box, planning to start training her to use it. Kurt and I are reading and Keira and her mates are cosily ensconced around the room, dozing. I keep glancing over at the box and moments later am amazed to see the tiny kitten climbing up the cardboard cliff and flopping down onto the floor, heading straight for the sand tray. Kurt and I watch, fascinated, as this resolute black furry creature climbs in, digs a hole, does her business and spends ages covering it up. But she can't even lap! So much for planning to train her. How I underestimated her species. She goes back to her box and curls up 'a little ball of fluff'.

Keira adopts the new kitten, which no doubt accounts for the kitten's rapid progress. Keira licks her and plays with her and sleeps with paws around her ... a ready-to-wear mother. We call her Sammy — her little face with the bright bright eyes reminds us of Sammy Davis Jnr. I keep her box beside our bed and feed her when she wants it. I quickly switched to a baby feeding bottle which works much better than the doll's bottle. Sam's tiny, earnest face looks up at me, resolute and independent yet curious about this huge creature gazing down. This feline species, never really tamed, never subservient — it always thrills me that we *can* bond.

The sun rises and sets, days come and go. Sammy grows, begins to lap one day and soon is eating. She is boss of the clan — never growing to the size of the other cats, long and sleek, her golden eyes holding theirs imperiously. Our big black part-Persian male, Aapje (which means 'little monkey' in Dutch) loves Keira. He is ecstatic at their first meeting and follows her everywhere. He is curious but in awe of Sammy. Heini, a real knockabout black and white male, takes to Sam with gusto but she keeps him at bay with her taut lithe body and kung fu stare.

Lazy summer days, furry bundles sprawling in hot sun pools. Heini bursts from somewhere, eager white whiskers spraying, and jumps on Sam, who is dozing and relaxed. In an instant he is whacked and Sam flies along the plank Kurt has run alongside the house for painting. She pauses at the end winding up, brief as a sigh, then becomes airborne and is over the fence onto the neighbours' flattish garage roof — plank to roof is some 3 metres or so.

Sam turns out to have a big serve of Burmese in her genes and becomes famous for her climbing and jumping feats. During renovations our neighbours removed their garage roof; one day I see Sammy soar through the air, heading for the non-existent roof and I feel that hopeless feeling of inevitability that descends upon us all at some time. I rush next door fearing the worst but Sam is on the ground completely unperturbed — after all, she always lands on her feet, the dynamic cat trick. No ill effects are noted. She's made of springs, says Kurt.

We never did find out where Sammy came from. Our back garden is fenced and gated so she could not have been dumped, and where was her mother? We never saw a strange cat anywhere. Someone suggested she may have been dropped by a bird of prey — the nick in her tail is consistent with this, but maybe she was dropped by an angel. How strong our bonds are with this beautiful cat, as sweet as angel breath.

Here we are in winter, the wind snarling around the house. Each cat has chosen his or her spot and curled up — my Russian hats are scattered around the room. Aapje makes a grand entrance, all long black spiky fur, his great plume of a tail up. Keira is on a chair, all ginger, black, white fluffy fur — how can one resist! Aapje heads over and squashes on with her. Heini is on his box tower, Sammy warm and soft and purry on my lap. Here we all are battened down in our cosy box — our spaceship — may it never land.

The phone is ringing — despite my desire to ignore it and to snuggle further into my pillow, I get up. It's my neighbour, Helen — Jani has been hit by a car.

I grab the torch and go down the stairs, squashing past the garbage bins to the fence where Helen's teenage son, Matt, tells me what happened. He heard a terrible thud and ran out and there was poor Jani staggering onto their block looking severely distressed, gasping for breath, eyes popping, almost choking yet desperately scrabbling up the narrow gap beside the house. Matt says the residents across the road had seen Jani desperately dodging at the last moment and his quick reflexes probably saved him, at least for now. Matt will take us the vet. Thank God for good neighbours!

I rush back inside to dress and grab the cat carrier. Jani is gasping in the dark and a strangled little meow comes out. I grab him and put him in the cage, the blackness seems to squeeze my heart.

Matt speeds us through the night. A very competent looking vet takes Jani — he is going to put him in an oxygen tent. The last I see is Jani's terrified face, his beautiful tiger face with broad orange-tipped nose and his robust little tabby-patterned body all hunched up. His eyes are full of fear, pleading with me. But now I have to trust.

In the morning I call the vet to hear the worst or the best or the mildly hopeful. She is rather pessimistic: she talks about taking his tail off and is worried about the swelling in his abdomen. Full of foreboding, I go straight over and bring Jani home. My friend Sue comes with me and seeing Jani so needing professional help we decide to take Jani to Sue's vet. On arriving, we realise they have just been flooded with other casualties and so off we go to the biggest veterinary place further off. This time we are lucky and their very experienced vets advise us to take Jani to a special animal hospital closer to the city. They also arrange for a lovely young couple, who run an animal ambulance service, to pick Jani up and soon he is on his way.

Over the next few weeks I call each day, often twice a day. At first they wait to see if Jani's ruptured bladder will heal itself. As I find out later, he had all sorts of drugs and intravenous fluids and so on. But it has been no use. Eventually they operate and sew up his tear, then trim off dead tissue around his kidneys. The operation had gone well.

Jani won't eat. The staff try all sorts of delicacies and I tell them what he likes. They decide he will be better at home. It is premature, but he must eat.

The pet ambulance brings him home. I am floating with happiness as they carry in the familiar cage. Clip the bolts, lift the metal lid and

Jani is out, taking me by surprise. I have forgotten that the wire door in the kitchen can be forced open by a desperate cat. He escapes into the garden. I eventually find him under the house, lying on the stacked timber. Instructions were to keep him quiet — he must have read them. There he stays for two days and finally comes out to nibble a little when I call him. He knows what's best, doesn't he? Next time when he ventures out, I grab him and take him inside. He settles on my lap and starts to purr. I once heard, on the television, a tiger purring; deep, very deep, and that's how it sounded.

The vet from the hospital rings, worried that Jani might still not be eating. I put the phone to Jani, to catch that purr, and the vet is reassured when I tell him that Jani is eating. About a week later I take him to the nearest vet, after all it's just a matter of taking out 'stitches'. The vet is an older lady (than average I guess) — very experienced, one felt, and competent. Apparently Jani needs a special instrument to take out the staples but never mind, she improvises, extracting one carefully — Jani never utters any protest, brave boy.

Home again, Jani sits looking so miserable that I take off the funny Elizabethan-looking collar he has been wearing to guard his wound from scratches. He shakes his head a little, thank goodness! I feel guilty at overriding the vet. But now it is the mindset that matters — especially important for this sensitive cat.

A few days after our vet trip and there is Jani on the back verandah. How small he looks in the background of thrusting trees and tumbling foliage. He is looking up, then side to side, at all the leafiness and sky and air, softly stirring. He seems to be taking in big breaths of contentment and smelling all the 'home' scents he had almost forgotten. His dreamy wonderment is palpable and transfers to me.

Six months have crept stealthily through our lives and there goes Jani up on the grey wall to check on the big big world and, even higher, onto the roof. Darling Jani is well again.

MARBLE AND BOBO

Allison Briggs

My 'boys' came into my life completely by accident. I didn't hope for it, I didn't plan it and to be perfectly honest I'm not even sure if I *wanted* it. I couldn't even tell you what effect they have had on my life, or describe my feelings for them if I tried.

Around two years ago I had been diagnosed with major depression. I was in my final year of a university degree, as well as working part-time to qualify for a career that I no longer liked or wanted. I withdrew from my friends, had no energy and lost enthusiasm for everything I had once enjoyed. My relationship was suffering. I had completely burnt out. I had always been a good student but I began to fall behind with my school work. Motivating myself to get out of bed became difficult. I didn't eat because I didn't have the energy to get up. Most days were spent sitting listlessly on my couch, staring into space for what seemed like hours. If I managed to get up, shower and make a cup of tea, I considered it to be a successful day.

Enter the cats.

Papuss and Katze were two seven-month-old ginger tabby littermates owned by a lovely girl called Kim, a friend of a friend. She told us that her neighbours had complained about her cats and her strata management had got involved. She'd been threatened with eviction. They had to go, and no one else had put their hand up to take them in. It was either us or the pound. These poor little kittens had been on Earth for less than a year and they'd already had a hard life. They'd been delivered to the Cat Protection Society with their litter when they were three weeks old, after being abandoned in a cardboard box near a shopping centre car park. They had since found a loving home with Kim, and now through no fault of their own they were facing a very uncertain future, even death.

To be honest, I think it was the pity that made me want to bring them in. I'd never owned a cat before. I'd go so far as to say that I didn't even *like* cats. I had no clue what I was doing, or why I'd agreed to do it, but before I knew it Papuss and Katze were loaded up into my car and coming home with my partner and me.

Papuss has beautiful mahogany marbled swirls on his back. I first looked at him and said, 'He looks like a marble cake.' In an instant, he was renamed. Marble. Katze proved a little bit more difficult to re-moniker. He was very cautious and aloof, yet at times he was so snuggly and affectionate. We named him Bobo after Mr Burns' much-loved (yet frequently abandoned) teddy-bear on *The Simpsons*. In a freakish coincidence we found out later that Bobo had been Kim's nickname for Katze when he was a tiny kitten.

I was amazed by their huge personalities. Bobo is a darling, snuggling up to us and yelping loudly for kisses and hugs. He also delights in falling asleep on our laps. He is a joy. Marble, on the other hand, is a macho alpha type. He is haughty and butch, and a bit of a bully. He constantly picks fights with Bobo, but he always loses. But deep down underneath that bully is a total sook, who cries and scratches at our bedroom door early in the morning and gives us deep, throaty purrs when we come out and say hello.

So in those days my boys were my companions. They were my lifeline. They kept me connected, they kept me engaged and they gave me a reason to keep on going when the future seemed hopeless.

Marble

Bobo

They made me smile. My partner and I bonded over them. Before I knew it, many people in our lives were referring to us as 'crazy cat people'. Not that we cared.

We had only had them for a month when I realised that I could no longer remember what my life had been like before we adopted them. Before, I'd had no idea how I was going to live with a cat. Now I wondered how I'd ever lived without one.

Wonderful things have happened since they came into our lives. I began to work again in another industry and have very gradually found work experience and direction. We've also adopted another little girl, Maisy, from the Cat Protection Society. My partner says that three isn't enough for him, and that he's aiming to adopt six. I guess we'll see.

We've now had our boys for over two years. Our curtains have been chewed out, the backs of our lounges have been gouged to shreds and our furnishings and clothes are constantly covered with cat hair.

And we wouldn't have it any other way.

MIA'S STORY

Helen and David Carroll

In May 2008 a burly delivery man discovered Mia wandering along Sussex Street in Sydney's CBD. She had a small tag around her neck which read: 'Great cat. Bad owner.' He knew he couldn't leave this small, thin creature on the streets, but he had a sick elderly cat at home himself so he did the next best thing — he phoned his mum and told her to expect a special delivery. That's how Mia found her way to Maria, one of the kindest women you are ever likely to meet.

Despite being fed and pampered, after a few days Mia's restless spirit took hold and she wandered down the road to take up residence in a shed where she watched our neighbour, Don, tinker on his old car for a couple of days. Don and his wife Christine then brought her around the corner to us and she's been with our family ever since.

Mia shares her house with Will, a seven-year-old boy, three fellow rescue cats — Fergus, Ella and Lily — and a 30-kilogram Rottweiler-cross rescue dog, Max, who is very wary of the feisty 3-kilogram ginger bundle with a growl like a lioness.

It was obvious when she joined our family that she had never experienced the usual creature comforts of home and she certainly wasn't used to being picked up for a cuddle. It has taken almost three years but now Mia likes nothing better than to curl up on our laps in the evening, even if she is quick to administer a little bite if the 'person cushion' dares to move.

She is an excellent hunter but so gentle with her prey that assorted skinks, snails, insects, cicadas and even magnificent butterflies can easily be released from her powder-puff mouth without a scratch or scar.

After being let out each morning Mia ascends to our roof where she watches the neighbourhood children assemble for the school bus. If ever she misses a day or two of 'rooftop supervision' due to inclement weather, we'll have a customary knock at the front door from a neighbour enquiring after her health. She traverses our small suburban block via rooftop and fence to peep into homes and spy on neighbours as they go about their lives — with open windows a particular temptation. She also loves to follow us around the garden, waiting to pounce from tiny hiding spots.

Great cat. Proud owners.

HANA

Nita Harvey

In November 1985 we adopted from the CPS a lovely little tabby and white kitten named Hana (Japanese for 'flower') and her littermate, a tortie and white we called Kumquat. Inseparable friends with completely different personalities, Kumquat liked to be nursed and cuddled but Hana preferred to just sit very close and purr. They were wonderful cats and got on very well with our two dogs.

We visited our son in Queensland in August 2002 and Quat and Hana boarded at the vet, where they had run of the clinic. Immediately on our return we went to pick them up. I noted that Hana didn't look very happy and the vet nurse said she hadn't been too happy but they were both purring at the sound of our voices. When home we released them from their carriers and Hana jumped out and ran down the front steps. When she reached the car where my husband was (still unpacking our gear) she collapsed. I went to her and she seemed lifeless. Panic stricken, we rushed back to the vet who pronounced her dead. The cause, he was sure, was a heart attack. Evidently she didn't feel well but only succumbed to her attack when she came back to the people and the home she loved.

RIP Hana 1985–2002

BELLA THE MOTHER CAT

Petra Dobrijevic

I arrived home from work one evening to find we had a 'new' cat — a young tabby who had been in our garden that afternoon stealing some bread we had left for the wild birds. When my mother opened the door to talk to the cat, she had climbed over the fence and raced out of sight, obviously terrified.

Every day after that, the cat would come into our garden. We began leaving cat food outside for puss and she would greedily scoff the lot but would disappear over the fence as soon as she noticed a human presence. This routine continued for some weeks when we noticed she had gained quite a lot of weight and then the realisation hit us — she was pregnant. We named her Bella.

It was a very cold winter. We continued to leave food and water for Bella but didn't see her for a few days. When she returned it was obvious that she had given birth to her litter. We suspected that she'd had her babies in a neighbouring yard as the house was vacant.

For a few weeks Bella would come to our verandah several times a day in search of food and water, and once satisfied would leave, returning, we presumed, to her kittens. We then had two weeks of bitterly cold weather, including torrential rain. At that time, Bella stayed on the verandah day and night, only scurrying away if we approached. With the harsh weather conditions and Bella's constant presence on our doorstep, we assumed the kittens had perished. We were very sad and felt sorry for poor Bella.

However, things were not as grim as they seemed. I was at work one day when my mother rang with good news: she had seen a small fluffy white kitten in our garden with Bella. When I arrived home that evening there were six little kittens under our jasmine bush with a very protective Bella hissing and growling at us. Bella had miraculously carried all six kittens over two 2-metre high fences onto our property — what a champion!

The rain was still falling heavily and Bella and her kittens were lying on wet soil. After making several unsuccessful attempts to rescue the kittens, we decided the best option was to place a large plastic bag with a soft jumper inside under the bushes, so they could all snuggle up and keep dry. We watched and waited for the kittens to go inside the bag but eventually we had to call it a night. As the rain kept pouring down that night, no one in our household got much sleep.

Early next morning, we looked inside the plastic bag: there were all six kittens sleeping peacefully — dry, warm and safe. Bella had slept on a blanket we'd placed in a box for her on the verandah. Things were looking up. Over the next few weeks we were able to pick up the kittens and cuddle them; some were more welcoming of our affection than others. Bella was always close by to make sure we did the right thing by her babies.

At about this time, I became quite ill and was forced to take extended leave from work. There were some days when I was unable to get out of bed and at these times, a visit from one of the kittens provided a welcome distraction. Merely having a kitten sitting on my feet or on my lap raised my spirits immeasurably. Feline companionship cannot be overestimated and I believe this played a significant role in my recovery. As my health improved, the kittens gave me a reason to get out of bed each morning and hours of entertainment as I observed their blissful, energetic play.

When the kittens were eight weeks old we contacted the Cat Protection Society for assistance with desexing and microchipping. A trap had to be set to catch Bella as she still would not let us touch her. The whole process went smoothly.

We grew very attached to the kittens and although we hadn't planned on expanding our cat family (well, not to such a large extent) we couldn't part with any of the kittens and kept the entire litter. The 'kittens' — Angel, Chloe, Sascha, Poppy, Tammy and Sandy — celebrated their fourth birthday recently and are much-loved members of our family.

As for Bella, she now tolerates us humans and is definitely the matriarch of the household. She will discipline her five daughters with a swipe or a hiss depending on her mood, but gives only love and attention to her son Sandy. The two are inseparable and constantly drape their tails across each other. Bella will occasionally allow me to rub her back when I am feeding her, but as soon as she realises it's me touching her she quickly moves away.

We don't know where Bella came from, or how people treated her before she found us, but we continue to show her love and affection. We know Bella loves us too — after all, she brought her precious babies to us and they all continue to enjoy life in the sunshine on our verandah.

DOGS, CATS AND
THE QUEEN OF THE DOORSTEP

Nerida Atkin

In 1998 my partner and I moved into our new home and were greeted by a friendly cat in the garden. I had grown up with cats and dogs all my life but my partner wasn't too fond of cats so he shooed her away. As the weeks went on the cat continued to visit, even sleeping on the doorstep. My partner continued to shoo her away, never nastily but he felt the owner needed to be more responsible. I started to feel sorry for the cat — she looked in good condition but something wasn't right. I saw her sleeping in the neighbour's yard and there were food bowls and a bed on their verandah. The cat continued to visit and run to me when I got home from work so I started leaving little titbits of food at the end of the driveway in a small bowl. Her visits became more frequent and she was even starting to win over my partner — I would see him giving her a pat but denying it! I visited the neighbours after a few months to enquire about her and they told me her story.

Her owners had lived in the house next to ours and when the cat was one year old, they moved out. They took her with them but she ran away and came back to the house they had lived in. They had moved four suburbs away and were quite shocked when they went looking for her and found her back at the old home. This happened three times. Her owner was renting out the original house so asked the tenants if she could stay, as she had an obvious attachment to the house. They agreed but as they had an old dog that lived inside and didn't like cats she would have to live on the front step. When I asked her name they told me they had never known her name so always called her 'Gett Outt' if she came in the house.

I came home and told my partner the cat's sad story and he was so upset he had been shooing her away that we decided to set her up a warm bed and food bowls on our verandah. As we didn't have any pets at the time I would let her inside now and then but she would always just have a quick look around, spray her scent around and then wait at the front door, letting out a little meow to be let back out. I started to treat her for fleas and worms and checked if she was desexed. Although 'Gett Outt' was a strange name she knew it and would run to you if you called it. I got her a nice collar and a name tag as well.

After ten years of living in our home, Gett Outt had become part of our family and was never at the neighbours' house. Every evening she would run to meet my car and be waiting on her bed in the morning to say hello. Our neighbours moved out and asked if we would take care of Gett Outt and we, of course, agreed.

We have now lived in the house for twelve years and by my calculations that makes Gett Outt fifteen years old. The local birds enjoy sharing her breakfast every morning and she loves to sunbathe in the garden. She is getting a little bit of arthritis now so even gets a heat pad in her bed on a cold night. She is truly a part of our family and both my partner and I are glad she adopted us ... the queen of the doorstep.

꧁ᜰ꧂

We had been fostering kittens for about three years and when our canine family member arrived we didn't know if we could continue. Piroska is

Gett Outt

a Hungarian Vizsla and we had decided she would be a mostly indoor dog, as our last dog had sadly been killed by a snake in our backyard and we didn't want the same to happen to her. As Vizslas are gundogs we weren't sure how she would react to a group of little five-week-old kittens running around. Any concerns we had were soon quashed when I brought home a young three-week-old kitten. Piroska, at this time now six months old, ran straight up to the kitten that was in my hand and started grooming her. She was so excited; she even brought the kitten a present (a shoe). The kitten didn't mind her at all and even groomed her back. As the kitten was so small I was bottle feeding her and Piroska would sit at my feet until the kitten was done, then clean the kitten's face and try to clean her bottom. If the kitten cried Piroska would run down the hall and find me, then whimper at me and look down the hall. She was only happy once I had seen the kitten was okay. She would also lie at the front of the carry cage the small kitten was in and sleep there, guarding her.

Since this initial introduction Piroska has become quite the foster mum. She always alerts me if the kittens are crying and sits in the bathroom with me when it's bath time, keeping an eye on the kittens and sometimes, I think, me to make sure I'm not hurting them.

Sadly not all the kittens we have fostered have made it and Piroska has now become an indicator for me, to almost tell me if the kittens are sick. I came home one day with a very young kitten who had been found abandoned. Normally Piroska will do her greeting at the door and bring the kitten a present; this time she merely sniffed the kitten and walked away. The kitten was with us for two weeks and not once did Piroska even enter the room the kitten was in. If she needed to go through the room she would run through and not look at the kitten. The kitten passed away from a neurological disorder. Did Piroska know? This has happened a number of times now and Piroska has acted the same with every kitten who has passed away. I now get a sick feeling if she doesn't greet them at the door.

Piroska has helped foster about 30 kittens in her three years of being a foster mum.

TIGER AND TINA

Maree Vesk

Once upon a time we had a kitten and my daughters named him Tiger. Though handsome like his namesake, there the similarity ended and we watched him grow into a gentle, sensitive and polite young lad. Then one afternoon on her way home from school my younger daughter found and brought home a starving, bedraggled little lump of fur who was soon christened Tina. Not much older than a kitten, she was so thin that only an implacable will to survive could have kept her alive.

After a brief stay at the local vet and with a health check, desexing and terminated pregnancy behind her, Tina came home bouncing with vitality — and an insatiable appetite. She explored the house, then ate. She slept on my daughter's bed, then ate. And at every opportunity, no matter how often she was reprimanded, she scoured the dining table for leftovers while Tiger watched on in horror at such an appalling lack of manners.

Poor Tina ate as though every meal would be her last. Meanwhile, Tiger had obviously given the matter some thought and decided that if this interloper could jump on the table, so could he; and so he squared his shoulders, took a deep breath — and leapt. He must have sensed my disapproval though I said nothing more than 'Oh, Tiger' for he looked mortified, jumped down and ran out and we did not see him again until that evening when he slunk in, a remorseful little cat.

But Tina had learned early in life that good manners would not fill her belly; that if she wanted to eat, she must fight. And it soon became clear that she was prepared to fight not just for herself but perhaps even more so for her friend, the gentle Tiger.

For a while we had to move to an apartment and while we lived there, Tiger and Tina stayed with my sister. Tina immediately made it clear to the next door neighbour, a brawny Persian called Bear, where the boundary was and made sure that Bear did not cross it (there was no physical fence). When (at first) Bear made unfriendly gestures towards Tiger, he had Tina to deal with. And Tina was tough.

Eventually we made our home in an inner Sydney suburb. Tiger pottered around the garage and did a bit of digging in the garden, while Tina checked out the local park. Time rolled on and we all got older but Tina's appetite remained undiminished. One day, after I had put their food outside as usual, I heard screeching and yowling and turned in time to see Tina chasing several cats away from Tiger's food and out of the backyard. As I was about to bring both cats and food inside I stopped, astonished. Tina was watching Tiger eat and did not touch her own food until Tiger had finished eating. A couple of days later I realised what Tina already knew: Tiger was ill. The vet said there was nothing he could do but assured me that Tiger was not in pain and would die peacefully when his time came.

They now ate in the kitchen, undisturbed by other cats, yet Tina still sat faithfully by Tiger's side. Each day Tiger grew weaker and each day Tina offered him her food and limitless love. When Tiger died, Tina cried for him and she searched for him; day and night she searched and cried. Then one day she did not come home. Her friend, her great love, had left this earth and she went to join him.

MY CAT, KITTY

Anneliese Harrison, aged 11

My cat is called Kitty. He is five years old, which makes him about 37 in cat years. He has short black hair and a lot of attitude. Kitty always demands food. He seems to think my mother is the primary food source so whenever she arrives home, he transforms from a nice, calm, satisfied cat to a 'I'm hungry, feed me now!' cat.

According to me, Kitty is very handsome, dashing and kind. I believe that I am Kitty's favourite because he sleeps on my bed and dribbles contentedly when he does.

Kitty is quite sour to other cats and to most people ... especially the vet! However there is one cat in particular that annoys him, a ginger tomcat who is very aggressive. Once they were fighting in our yard and the tomcat wouldn't leave. My father had to get the hose to scare him away. It was rather funny!

All in all I love my cat just as I love all the kittens and cats at the Cat Protection Society, and I hope I will get more.

FIVE CATS

Professor Richard Malik

As a child I had a sensitive nature (probably still do), which caused issues with the other kids at school. As a result I took comfort from my friendships with animals. I didn't grow up with cats. I spent a lot of time with a Fox Terrier-cross called Blossom who lived next door, and was attached to two special budgies while I was growing up. (My parents never let our family have a cat or a dog.) Later I worked in a horse riding school and got to own my own horse. So it wasn't a surprise to my family that I became a vet. But on reflection it was probably a really dumb thing for me to do, as I cope badly with grief and I grieve for many of my patients. It makes for a troubled life, especially if you concentrate on treating difficult cases, as there is always a deal of sorrow mixed up with the joy. However, I can't adequately describe the satisfaction I feel when I get one right for the animal. It's what keeps me going as a vet: seeing the relief and happiness on the family's faces as their pet recovers.

The vet course at the University of Sydney in the 1970s didn't teach me much as I wanted to know about cats, but it did teach me the value of knowledge and fundamental principles for understanding and fighting diseases. I didn't really get to know much about cats until 1983 when Karen, the vet nurse at Woden Animal Hospital, got me to take on a black and white ex-tomcat called Kiwi — he was named after the New Zealand horse Kiwi, who won the Melbourne Cup on the day the cat was surrendered to the practice. Kiwi taught me a lot about cats: that they make friendship on their own terms, and how they like sharing time and space with us humans. Looking back, it was funny learning about the feline–human bond in my twenties, but then again my personal view is that kids should grow up with dogs and graduate to cats when they have developed more refined tastes!

I only had about seven years with Kiwi. He developed malignant lymphoma in 1990. After I put him to sleep I was beside myself. I foolishly didn't wait sufficient time to grieve and I tried out a couple of cats, but none filled the void. One, Ginge, ended up with my mum, and another, Lucky — well, we became mates but that took years.

Around that time I was studying a type of muscular dystrophy in Devon Rex cats, a breed I hadn't had much to do with, and took on a ginger boy called Baron (as in the Red Baron) who was bred by a gentle breeder, John Sternbeck. Baron missed out on finding a home as a young kitten, and I got him when he was about five months old. Baron and I hit it off — and finally I had another cat who touched my soul. I kept Lucky, and over the years I learned how special he was too, but that took much longer — he was a very special cat with a very gentle nature.

When I ended up with the two cats, Baron and Lucky, I had the joy of seeing their relationship evolve and mature. Initially they were rivals, but they were mates too. Baron was a cheeky little fellow (quite typical for the breed), feisty, independent and strong-willed. Lucky was a gentler and more even-tempered silver tabby, but they became friends and developed a special bond over the years.

When they were both about ten, I got a very cute CPS kitten called Miss Binks — a very naughty tortie. Very affectionate (in-your-face affectionate) but very cheeky. This experiment in succession planning didn't work out quite the way I had hoped — because Binky really hit it off with Lucky, who looked after her like a father or older brother (sorry to be so anthropomorphic, but cats do that to me). Needless to say, Baron was annoyed big time! Indeed, it took over two years for him to come to accept her, but he never really did completely.

Lucky lived till he was about eighteen. I never knew exactly how old he was, as he was an ex-blood donor cat from the veterinary teaching hospital. Baron lived till he was nineteen. Two score years is a big part of your life. Although it was really tough to lose them, I took comfort from knowing they lived long, full and contented lives. They went everywhere with me: to my farm, skiing (well, not quite — but they were smuggled into an apartment at Jindabyne for a few weeks every year) and to my brother's 'shack' at Pearl Beach (it's actually bigger than my house).

It was certainly smart thinking to have Miss Binks, as I had formed a special bond with her by the time it was time to say goodbye to Lucky, and then Baron. I am sure that made their passing easier for me.

The latest acquisition is a cute black and white moggy called Obi. (I have a *Star Wars* Jedi thing going: Obi is short for Obi-Wan Kenobi, while Miss Binks is named in honour of Jar Jar! I guess that makes me Yoda.) He is pretty special too, but just as Miss Binks used to annoy Baron when she was young, now it's Obi's turn to upset Binky's Jedi karma. I am sure they will settle down soon — a warm heater seems to cause a frenzy of mutual grooming, but I wish Obi would learn not to hijack her in the corridor.

One thing I have learned over the years is that every cat is different. When you lose one you really feel you want their qualities in the next cat, but it's actually far better to get a different make, colour and model. That way it's easier to preserve the special memories about the ones that you have lost. I am also absolutely certain that we don't need pedigree cats, even though I loved my Devon to bits. People think they can predict the personality and behaviour of their pet based on pedigree. To a degree, this is so. But there is a huge price — as well as fixing the shape, colour and personality traits of the breed, you invariably fix deleterious genes that contribute to disease. So even though I love all cats, I am completely in favour of breaking down breed boundaries and embracing genetic diversity.

Another thing I learn from owning cats is that cats do best if fed natural food (raw meat on the bone) as a substantial component of their ration, and that a diet solely consisting of dry cat food, although convenient, is *no way* to feed a creature that evolved as an obligate carnivore.

When you see lions and tigers it doesn't take long to realise that we love cats because they have not been completely domesticated (don't you adore that streak of independence they possess?), and that even though they share our houses, beds and lives there is still a 'big cat' not that far under the skin of every domestic short hair.

RAGS, GIZMO AND BLACKIE

Sandy Moss

I grew up on a farm where the only cat we had was a tomcat (never desexed) and he was solely to catch mice and rats in the feed shed. He did get fed every day and patted when he let us but he was not what you'd call a lovable cat. We also had a kelpie. They tolerated each other but the cat would take every opportunity to tease the dog.

When the oats were about a foot high, the cat would hide in the middle of the paddock and move the oats. The dog would then creep in to see what was happening. Next there would be blood-curdling screams and the dog would rush out with his nose ripped to shreds.

The cat, who was called Puss, was known all around the district as the father of many kittens. Back in those days, the '60s, not many people desexed their cat or dog and they were allowed to roam the neighbourhood day and night. Puss lived to a ripe old age and for a long time afterwards we were without a cat.

I decided that it was time to get another and a friend told me about these Siamese kittens that another friend had bred so we made arrangements to go and get one. The place was miles away from us so off we set one morning with a cardboard box to put the kitten in. I'd decided to get another male and this time get it desexed as by now I was older and wiser!

We arrived at the farm and the friend took us to the garage/granny flat where the mum and kittens were living. As we were going through the doorway into the room my friend said, 'Quick, get in and close the door.' I didn't realise why until I saw these tiny little things tearing all over the place. It turned out that the mum was very friendly but because the kittens had not been handled much they were totally *wild*! My friend asked whether I wanted a male or female but after an hour of trying to catch them I said I'd take whatever we could catch. Eventually I caught one and this gave me my first taste of that excruciating pain of a cat's bite. They might only have been eight weeks old but boy could they bite. I was bitten on both hands, had blood flowing freely but no way was I letting go of my prize. My friend drove the one hour home and I clutched that kitten for dear life, by now wrapped up in a bundle of rags, as the kitten still tried to bite me.

I had already decided before we left home that the kitten would stay in my bedroom until big enough to be let out, so in went the kitten with food and water and the door firmly closed. It took me a few days to get the kitten to come to me and be handled and I still didn't know the kitten's sex, but eventually I discovered she was a girl and I named her Rags. She was an absolutely beautiful cat and gave me my first experience of how great cats are. I loved her dearly and she lived to a ripe old age. She lived with two Dobermans, a German Shorthaired Pointer and later on an ex-CPS adult named Tina.

When I worked as a welfare officer for CPS I often saw very sad cases of neglect and cruelty and the following story involves both of those things. Around 1995 I was in the office at Enmore when a young man came in with a Devon Rex kitten. It was an un-desexed male and about sixteen weeks old. He had bought the kitten for a friend as a present and they had had him for about six weeks before deciding they didn't want him anymore so he thought the best thing to do was to surrender him. We took the kitten in and sent him over to Concord Animal Hospital for assessment. I noticed at the time that his eyes were practically stuck shut with gunk and he was also sneezing a lot. When he was examined by the vet he was found to have cat flu and had a problem with one of his tear ducts and also had several marks on his back consistent with cigarette burns. Someone had been butting out their cigarettes on his back. We were all horrified to think that this poor little kitten had been through hell because he wasn't wanted.

Well that changed when my partner Alice saw him. We already had five cats so what was one more, she said. She had always wanted a Devon Rex so after treatment and desexing we purchased him and he came home with us and was named Gizmo. He quickly became pals with Max, the youngest of the five, but the other cats regarded him with utter contempt and couldn't stand him. He wanted to be the only cat in the house so caused havoc whenever he could. Regardless of that we both loved him. He gave love all the time; that seemed to be his mission in life. When we brought foster kittens home for a few weeks, he would take them under his wing and look after them. He loved those kittens whereas the other cats always had a hissy fit and ran off when a kitten was sighted.

He was very protective of his backyard and would fight any cat that wandered in. The only problem was that he always came off second best and then ran off and hid for 24 to 48 hours, nursing his wounds. He would not come to you after a fight but would stay silent in whatever hiding place he had found. We would spend hours looking for him but when he was ready he would come out and get his wounds attended to.

Gizmo had a great life with us for ten years and was much loved, which I always hoped made up for the first sixteen weeks of his life.

On another occasion during my time with the CPS I was asked to participate in a segment for the television show *Better Homes and Gardens* with Dr Katrina Warren. The idea was 'Do big male cats (e.g. lions) and small cats (domestic) have similar habits?' At the time Alice and I had six cats at home so I was the lucky one chosen.

The day of filming finally arrived and the crew turned up at our house — Dr Warren, the cameraman, the sound man and the director. By that time of day all the cats had taken themselves off to various parts of the garden and house for a snooze. I forgot to mention that at the time we had a daily visitor from up the road. He was a black and white un-desexed young male about five or six months old and he used to come every day and sleep on a small table on the rear patio. I'd even put a towel there for him so he'd be comfy. We had no idea who he belonged to but our cats didn't seem to mind him and Vita (one of our desexed girls) was positively smitten. She loved him. We nicknamed him Blackie.

So the camera was set up and the filming started. Firstly Katrina did her preamble and after a few takes it was time to grab a male cat. I picked Reg as he was the most laidback cat of all time. Nothing worried him (well, usually). Katrina was holding Reg and was talking away to the camera when Reg suddenly spotted the big furry thing, the microphone, being held by the sound guy. All hell broke loose as he fled. After I found him again (he was always a sucker when you called him!) several more attempts were made to film him before he was unceremoniously dumped as the star of the show as by that time Blackie had turned up for his daily visit. As he was un-desexed he was ideal for the story and so won himself a part in the show. He behaved impeccably and even sprayed on the wall (much to Katrina's delight).

When the segment was aired, there was Blackie as the star of the show.

KISU

Milla Peltola

We adopted Cuddles (who now goes by the name Kisu) one and a half years ago and since getting her she has changed completely from an anxious cat to an extremely affectionate one.

We initially fell in love with her when her photo was posted on CPS's Facebook page. At the time we had discussed getting a cat in the near future and it wasn't our plan to get a cat so soon, but after seeing her photo I 'convinced' my partner that we could at least go and have a look at her.

When we arrived at the CPS we asked to see Cuddles and were taken upstairs. She was eating and she looked as adorable as in the photos. Our image of her soon changed, however, when she exited her cage and started viciously hissing at us. She then started walking around and kept hissing at all the other cats, who immediately ran away from her. She was pretty much hissing at everything and the moment we approached her she tried to swipe us. The staff at the CPS advised us against going too close.

They told us Cuddles had been at the CPS for as long as ten months; whenever someone took an interest in her she started swiping and hissing and would therefore not be picked. Even my mother-in-law asked

Kisu

me whether this was a good idea and tried to show me other cats. But I said no, we were here to get Cuddles and I remember saying that once she had a loving family and gained trust I was sure we could get rid of her hissing and swiping. So against all rational thinking, we agreed to take her home. The CPS staff member had to get her into her cat carrier as we were too scared to even approach her let alone touch her!

I always thought it would take time for Cuddles to change but she changed completely the moment we brought her into the house. When she first came out of her cat carrier my mother-in-law reached her hand towards her and, after thinking she would get a huge swipe, we were amazed that Cuddles welcomed the affection and started to purr.

Her change continued; she started watching television with us on the couch and slowly made her way to sleep in the bed with us every night. She quickly became really attached to us and would demand affection and tummy rubs by rolling onto the floor the moment she saw us. She would recognise our voices and the moment we'd get home she would start crying for affection. But she still changed to a reserved cat whenever we had guests over and even though she would be curious she would hide and avoid any contact as best she could.

It didn't take too long for Cuddles to get rid of her anxiety altogether. Nowadays she loves having people over as she realises there are more hands to pat her and she will get more attention. She still sleeps in the bed with us, literally on us, and wakes us up around 5 a.m. to pat her. If she does not get noticed, she will walk onto your pillow and start crying in your ear and throw herself on your face. One morning when we ignored her cries for affection we suddenly heard a loud banging. I got up to look and Cuddles was hitting her paw against our walk-in wardrobe creating this noise while looking towards us in the bed to see if it was waking us up.

Nowadays we never hear a hiss from Kisu, as she's now known, and she never ever swipes anyone. She is an important part of the family and it's hard to imagine home life without her. I just want to thank CPS for sticking with her for a year and not giving up on her finding a home. And also to remind all cat lovers to not always go for cute kittens — try a cat with personality like our Kisu.

MISCHIEF AND DEUS'S TALE

Penelope Wardle

One evening my seven-year-old Labrador cross, Mischief, woke me up barking at a noise in the garden. Armed with a torch we went outside to find the intruder was a very tiny tabby kitten (about six weeks old) looking for food in the rubbish bin. We took her in and fed her 'just for the night' and then put her outside the door the following morning — of course she was still there in the evening and for the next sixteen years. This little kitten became Deus.

Mischief was a very maternal dog (a rescue herself) and happily accepted all the various stray dog and cat rescues that passed through the house, but she seemed to form a special bond with Deus and in many ways brought her up as if she was a puppy. As a result Deus would come on our dog walks, happily sit on the back seat of the car on drives and generally preferred dogs to other cats. When this latter preference led inevitably to the odd patch of trouble, her protector Mischief would step in to rescue Deus and take her back to safety.

As the years went on Mischief slowed down and spent more time sitting in the sun (or on the sofa) than playing or walking, her friend Deus often by her side or giving her a quick head butt on her way to some activity. One evening Deus started an unearthly yowling and we found Mischief had had a blackout and fallen down the back stairs. A veterinary exam showed she had a benign tumour which was pressing on her lungs. While benign, as she was then seventeen and the tumour was not operable we decided to take her home with us for as long as she was comfortable. We all moved downstairs and started to sleep and eat in the lounge room to be with her — but Deus truly became her shadow and the roles of protector and provider became reversed.

Deus slept by her side, brought her mice (generally ignored but it's the thought that counts) and when Mischief sat by the open door to get fresh air and sun Deus became the protector sitting in front of the door on the step, warning off any that came to close. On the final day Deus seemed to sense it was Mischief's time and refused to move off her friend's bed, lending warmth, support and purrs on the final night.

After Mischief had gone Deus visibly grieved and would not move off Mischief's bed except for toileting — we even had to feed her next to the bed. After a few weeks had passed she finally moved from the bed but followed us around whenever we went in or out of the room, not at all like her former independent self. She stayed like this until April when we acquired a (then) small black and white puppy, Scamp — it was love at first sight and Deus now had a baby 'Mischief' to sleep and play with, so a happy ending. Do cats truly form bonds — do they grieve, do they love? If Mischief and Deus are any example then for me that answer is a resounding yes.

KIT'S STORY: A CAT IN SERVICE

Mary Wolfla

I meet Kit on a rainy day at the Cat Protection Society. I had been volunteering once a week for about six months at the cat shelter, cleaning litter trays, washing cat dishes and socialising with cats of all kind and colour. At the time I was not looking to adopt a cat; I was new to Sydney, having recently moved over from the United States. Then one day while cleaning cat dishes my world changed. I spotted a new arrival at the cat shelter. His name was Kit. He was seven years old and had a handsome kitty face with champagne and white coloured fur. Some might describe him as 'chubby' or 'pleasantly plump' — he definitely was one of the largest cats I had ever seen. As soon as I was done with the cat dishes that day I spent the afternoon cuddling Kit; it was love at first sight. That night I went home and convinced my husband that we needed to adopt this handsome cat. He came by the shelter and quickly agreed that Kit needed to be a member of our family.

I knew Kit was a special cat from the moment we met, but when he first came home we went through a teething period. He tested me and, in my own way, I guess I tested him, too. Slowly he began to learn he could truly trust me and my husband, and after a few months Kit became confident that he had found his forever home.

About a year after adopting Kit my husband and I moved to Perth. Kit travelled with us, and is more at home in Perth than we could have ever imagined. We have started to suspect that Kit is a natural born West Australian cat.

Kit

When I arrived in Perth I started a job as an events coordinator for a senior citizens' day centre. The centre is a place for seniors to have a meal, socialise, go on weekly day trips and order in-home services such as cleaning and gardening. Many of the senior spoke to me about the cat or dog they could no longer have because they now had to live in housing that did not allow pets. This left a big hole in the hearts of many of my senior clients. After hearing these sad stories I decided Kit needed to come visit the seniors at the day centre.

The big day came and Kit and I travelled to work together. I set Kit up in a spare room in our facility. The room was set up like a bedroom, with a day bed and a big sunny window. As the seniors arrived for lunch and daily activities I told them Kit was visiting and they could go and see him. My senior clients were excited! Kit's visit to the day centre had been on the social calendar for a couple of weeks and it proved to be a popular event. One at a time I took each person to visit Kit in the spare room. I was impressed with Kit's patience and immediate affection for my senior clients. He jumped off the bed and greeted each person as they entered the room, then my clients got to sit on the bed and give Kit pats and cuddles, as well as some of Kit's favourite kitty treats. Naturally Kit loved all the attention.

Being able to spend time with Kit deeply affected many of my clients. Some had tears of joy, others of sadness for the pet they could no longer have. Being able to spend time with an animal was also healing for many of my clients, lifting their sprits and helping them to forget their physical pain and worries for a little while. Over the course of the day Kit visited with over 25 senior citizens, and many other staff and volunteers. Kit was gentle and accepting of everyone that day. He went far beyond the call of duty. In the late afternoon Kit took a nap and sunbathed in the big sunny window of the day centre. He had a great day!

After Kit's visit my clients told me how much they enjoyed spending time with him. The positive effects of Kit's visit lasted for many weeks. Many of them told stories of their own pets they had had as children or in their adult lives, sharing funny stories and bonding over a mutual love of animals. Being able to bring Kit to the day centre was a rewarding and heart-warming experience. In the end I can't take any of the credit for this wonderful day. Kit did all the work, and the way he interacted with my senior clients was just magic.

MUCH LOVED MOGGIES

Patricia Baker

My earliest recollection of a cat in the family was one that my older brothers had rescued (so I am told) by going through barbed wire at Bondi Beach towards the end of World War II. They had seen a bag washed up by the tide and went to investigate and found a half-drowned grey tabby kitten. He was rushed home and given the best first aid as my mother was also 'animal mad'. When he recovered we named him Moses — no bulrushes nor basket, but certainly a reminder of the biblical figure!

I am not sure how long Moses was part of the family and his probable end was at the hands of a local poisoner who hated cats and poisoned every cat we ever owned while we lived in those flats. We left there when I was aged fourteen.

I owned my first cat as an adult while I was working in the office of the famous Glass Works at Waterloo. After a long weekend, on opening the store room door the paymaster found that a factory cat had been locked in there and had produced three kittens — I imagine the paymaster's language and tone were the reason the poor little mother took off. As the RSPCA was then situated across the road, the kittens were to be taken over and 'put down'.

My love of cats had already become known around the factory. I was therefore told about the kittens and took them over the road to get instructions on a formula to feed the three-day-old kittens. I took them home and started feeding them via syringe. I would take them each day to work in a 'bucket bag' complete with hot water bottle. As luck would have it, we had car problems during this time and I once had to travel home by train. Imagine peak-hour train travel with me feeding one kitten, another stranger feeding the second kitten and a dear old man pacifying the third kitten!

The next addition came out of the blue. A lady walked into the office and said she had just found a kitten in the Tommy Smith stables (at Kensington) and someone had said I would take it — I never did find out who that was! The kitten, whom I named Soot, was a tiny black and white bit of fur and I went back to the syringe/goat milk formula. After about two weeks she seemed to develop dandruff so I took her to the vet. 'Oh dear,' he said. 'She is full of ringworm and you have long hair. Leave her and I will put her down.' No way, I thought — the kitten was put on tablets and so was I. She lost all her fur and when it grew back, it was black, long and silky. She had to spend the next few weeks closed in the main bathroom and I had to wear a special gown to feed her — but Soot and I sure bonded!

Another addition was Rastus. Rassy was quite wild. He suddenly appeared in a tree in the front yard — I heard this yowling and there he was. He seemed to spend most of his time high up there and at dusk I would put a small quantity of food at the foot of the tree and leave him. It took me nearly six months to gradually move the food up to the front porch and almost as long to get him to allow me to pat him. His back was like minced steak and the vet said it was probably from a fight with a possum. To help it heal I started putting a cortisone tablet into his food and gradually the skin settled. After about another year I was able to put a tranquiliser in his food and my girlfriend who was a vet, de-sexed him on the dining room table! He was a joy and so very lovable. Unfortunately due to the life he had led, his kidneys gave way after about four years. I wished he had been able to enjoy his new life for longer.

Another strange addition was Emma. About to enter church in the city on Saint Patrick's Day, I came across a cat sitting by the door. One doesn't often see a beautiful long-haired cat in the middle of the city sitting at a church door — something is wrong, I thought — so I enticed her in and she stayed near me. I had to get to work at Waterloo and had nothing to put her into so I rang the housekeeper at the presbytery and asked her to feed the cat until I could pick her up on Sunday, which I did. She had fur off her paw and had obviously just been to the vet. I advertised for her owner but got no response, so she joined the clan.

My last cat to be put to sleep lived until she was seventeen and was my shadow. If I was upset, Melody would come and sit on my knee and put her paw onto my face, making little cat noises — she knew my every mood and was always there for me. Pork, Ginge, Soot, Mignonne, Edward, Smudge, Melody, Seymour, Rastus, Emma, Monty, Manselle, Gina, Sophie and Annie — so many much-loved cats and each time their lives have ended I have had to see them die in my arms via an injection and it never gets easier. My garden has all their graves plus those of three dogs. My dogs were my dogs but my cats were my family.

Cats have always been a major part of my life and have given me such joy and comfort. Each of those little cats mentioned above was discarded by someone who missed out on such a lot of joy. I can understand why the Egyptians worshipped them as they certainly seem to possess a certain mystery that dogs, as lovable as they are, do not have. I currently have five cats — all from welfare, taken in at various stages of their lives and my hope is to try to make their lives happier than that from whence they came.

Each time a little feline life ends, a fragment of my soul goes with them and when I too die I am certain that all these fragments will come back to me and we will be together again. For my grave I have left instructions for the inscription: 'No heaven will heaven be unless my cats are there to welcome me.'

PIPER

Simon Hawkins

Growing up in a small town in Queensland, I was a loner at a young age and happy to be one. One of my first recollections of the happy times my family and I had growing up with pets was of our tabby named Jeremy. I clearly recall him being my first and only friend for quite some time; whether he felt the same way was another matter entirely! Twenty years later, and as a grown-up big city dweller, I got used to living without pets, given the restrictions placed on rental tenants these days. Well, I guess I could have had a bird but it's not really the same now, is it? But deep down I've missed the experiences and memories you gain by owning a special pet to call your own.

When I met my partner it didn't take me long to realise that this was someone who could definitely benefit from the well-published positive influences cats can exert. Their ability to lower blood pressure and associated stress levels was of particular interest! I think he got the hint, and surprised me by suggesting, out of the blue, that we pay a visit to the Cat Protection Society one weekend. Personally, I'm still haunted by the day I paid a visit to a pet pound in Brisbane many years ago; the sounds the animals made were like none other I'd heard. It was as if they knew their fate, and it wasn't good. I wasn't sure if I was going to experience more of the same at the CPS but I firmly believe that if you really crave owning an animal, you must try to rescue one from the last bastion of hope that places like this provide.

When we arrived at the CPS I was pleased to see that handfuls of caring, warm, genuinely excited people were spending time playing with the kittens in the courtyard. Having grown up with a number of family cats over the years, I knew the kind of personality our feline needed to have. We wanted a confident but calm kitten. One we could play with but who would also be happy being still when the time was right. The courtyard was littered with about seven or so kittens, all a different colour and all about six weeks old. Some were darting here and there, others were play-fighting each other atop climbing frames, and some were asleep. Our little man entered our lives ever so calmly. Not fazed by the excitement, a black, grey and white striped kitten strode up to where I was standing. At 190 centimetres tall and close to 100 kilograms in weight I stood against the glass wall of the enclosure, out of the way, mindful of how easy it might have been for me to step on one of the babies and not even know it. But looking down at the little fella at my feet, he didn't seem bothered by me or my size. So I crouched down and gently picked him up. He was so calm I initially thought something was wrong with him, but then the purring started. Holding him up to my chest, he calmly reached up to my shoulder and climbed up, perching himself, happy to have the best seat in the house.

You know you've found the pet for you when you dare not put him down for fear that someone else will take him home. So after half an hour of bonding, my partner Anthony and I made the decision to adopt this confident little fur ball. Once in the car I was startled by this puss's behaviour again, or lack thereof. He was so calm, apart from insisting we improve his view by letting him out of his cat carrier.

Once settled at home, it didn't take our little one long to get acquainted with his new surroundings. But again, his concentration was focused on being up high. Whether it was being perched on the bedhead, on the back of the couch, on the breakfast bench, inside the wardrobe (the highest shelf, of course), the kitchen sink — whatever could afford him the best view. So when it came time to name our little explorer, Anthony and I looked at each other with the same

Piper

thought in mind: what title personified his fixation with heights? I've been crazy about aviation and flying for most of my life so I naturally gravitated towards the names of aircraft, so we thought: Airbus, Boeing, McDonnell Douglas ... Obviously commercial airliners just weren't designed with cute names. So we pondered light aircraft: Beechcraft, Cessna, and finally ... Piper! So Piper it was.

Fast forward nearly three months and it still seems that our days are entirely occupied by Piper, in the best possible way. I've rediscovered the genuine sense of warmth you can feel having a feline companion around and, importantly, Anthony has found a sense of calm and peace at home. Okay, so that is sometimes interrupted when Piper decides to do his business in the bathroom sink but, hey, he is still a baby. As I remind Anthony, Piper will be an adult cat in less than six months and when he lays curled up in a ball for twenty hours a day we will look back at the days we ran around the apartment on poop scoop duty with affection. Anthony has developed a genuine emotional bond with our kitten, something which we also saw in the volunteers at the CPS as they went about their duties. Those guys and girls deserve a very special mention — without people like them looking out for the welfare of cats and kittens, I shudder to think of the outcome. Their dedication is infectious, and very much visible, so a very special thank you to you.

THE STORY OF LUCKY/CLOVER

Mandy Stewart

I needed a cat. A special cat. A cat who could be independent and brave and, when necessary, bossy. I was the very proud owner of a lovely miniature Dachshund, Cinnamon, who was in desperate need of a pet companion and friend. A second dog was simply not an option, but I know that, contrary to popular myth, cats and dogs can get along. I just needed the right cat for the job.

I visited the Cat Protection Society and met some of the cats looking for a new home. The big bossy black and white boy looked promising, but then I thought he might end up bullying the dog! Then I met Lucky — she was both brave and timid, as if she couldn't make up her mind. A bit like me. I ummed and ahhed before deciding that Lucky was the cat for me (and Cinnamon).

Bringing Lucky home brought about two immediate things. First, a name change. Lucky became Clover. Second, a shock to the household dynamics. Cinnamon was completed enamoured of the new addition to the family, but I couldn't say the same for Clover. It was a strange new environment, with a small and excited dog trying to make friends all the time. A couple of interesting days (the 'getting to know you' stage) followed. There was a bit of sitting in the hand basin ('Ha ha, you can't get me now') and some hisses and a few swipes. A few days, however, was all it took. Before the week was out, Cinnamon had calmed down and Clover had settled in. They were nose to nose and friend to friend, much to my relief and happiness.

Today, sixteen months later, they are well-adapted pet siblings. They share a bed in the winter months and play together around the house. The dog chases the cat; the cat gets up high, and has been known to launch herself in an attempt to land on the dog's back. That has met with only mixed success. The moments I love the most are when they are curled up together in front of the fire and take turns grooming each other. Particularly when Cinnamon just lies on her back and Clover licks her as she would a kitten.

The pitter patter — no, actually it's more like a pounding — of eight paws thundering on the wooden floorboards does bring a smile to my face, and I know that I made the right decision in choosing Clover. She has enhanced my life and Cinnamon would be lost without her.

KITTY BAXTER,
MY VERY SPECIAL GIFT

Allana Flynn-O'Neile

Kitty Baxter, Kitty Baxter tiny little one, born and abandoned and still not two days old. In long grass you lay, discovered just as you were about to be mown down. You were so small within my hand; they said it was not possible for you to live. Do not become attached, they said, as you would leave us soon. In your cries, however, I felt a spirit kindred to my own. There seemed in you a determination that deserved a chance. Your chance, for in those first few moments we had already become attached.

For many weeks we scheduled and charted your needs, every two hours day and night. You shared our lives wrapped in my beanie, your home a shoe box. Whenever and wherever we went, the shoe box went too — you nestled within. My glasses next to you looked as if they belonged to a giant. So perfect you looked, oh tiny little kitten. Your tiny ears, closed eyes, clear nails and little black nose. A nose surrounded by long black whiskers, like pins on a cushion. A perfect specimen. Like a small porcelain knick-knack, so cute you could be placed upon the mantlepiece. But as small as you were, your mouth opened wide with your cries for help. Your cries were loud and demanding, but time and patience were needed to convince you to drink. Throughout the night we would wait anxiously for you to cry out, whereupon the bottle would be gently squeezed and pressed against your mouth. But no, stubborn, you would refuse to drink. Many a time it would have been much easier to just give up during those long late-night hours and return to our bed. However, patiently we would wait and when hope was almost gone you would guzzle down that nectar.

Kitty Baxter

Then one day as the shoe box was opened — surprise, as two little blue eyes opened wide. Those bright eyes gazing up at us, now the world for you to see! Now you could watch as we tempted you, for what before you could only sense. Your determination now ruled strong. And not long after, another surprise came in the early hours one morning: suddenly you started to purr. Yes you were growing, from a struggling newborn to a small kitten. A small kitten eagerly becoming a beautiful young cat. A very determined cat! Those blurry blue eyes were now lovely shades of green. Your shoe box was replaced by a larger shoe carton, a Baxter boots shoe carton. Nameless you had been called Kitty, for weeks Kitty. Kitty had survived and now needed a name. Your master declared: 'Her name is Baxter — Kitty Baxter!'

And so, Baxter, this is your story. Your black fur is now tinged with gold. Yes a moggy, with the temperament of a tortie. Most of all, you were a gift to us — a gift given to me by your master. Together we fought for your chance to survive. The three of us, our determination now complete. You were to be the last gift he gave me, your master, who was taken most suddenly in the early months of your life. Now there is just you and I, Kitty Baxter, and you are my very special gift.

MY CAT, BEAR

Harry, aged 9

My cat is a lovely fluffy bear-looking cat. He sleeps on my bed at night and tries to bite my toes. He has a green collar, a green ball and a little green house.

He loves to play with my Lego. He pushes it around the floor and tackles my dog Bonnie's head. He likes to climb the tree in the garden. If you scratch his tummy he'll bite your hand.

Bear has little white paws and brown hair that sticks out like a fluffy ball that has been running in the air and the air pushes it into the shape of a ball.

He loves being chased by Bonnie. When we have our bath Bear jumps up next to us and we put bubbles on his head.

CATMATE AND SHADOW

Wendy Allan

Every cat is so special and beautiful. How lucky we are to find that a dear little feline wants to communicate with us, to share their world with us. Such inspiring little creatures are cats. They want to spend time with us, to play with us, to engage with us in so many endearing ways.

I first knew Catmate when, as an utterly charming kitten, he used to visit from his home next door. He was of course a very welcome visitor and, as it happened, a very regular one. Sometime later, while he was still quite a young cat, due to a change in circumstances next door and by agreement he came to be my very own cat.

Catmate was a gorgeous ginger male cat. Right from the start I was totally captivated by him; he was without doubt an enormously engaging feline. To Catmate, life was just one great big adventure after another; he had an enormous zest for fun and adventure and a lively interest in whatever was going on around him. Immensely friendly, affectionate and outgoing — that was Catmate, each and every day. There was such a strong sense of connection between us; we developed a mutual understanding of one another, a gift of the spirit. I adored him, loved playing with him and loved watching whatever tricks and antics he would get up to.

One of my greatest memories of my early years with Catmate is how he showed such excitement when I came home from work in the late afternoons, watching out for me and rushing to meet me in the driveway, dashing across the lawn to let me know how thrilled he was to see me, his fur a blaze of gorgeous ginger in the afternoon light. I was always equally excited to come home and share such special times with him too, of course. Rich blessings were mine! He was just so companionable. He loved sitting with me in the evenings, just being part of occasions. Naturally he also settled down on my bed at night and slept peacefully there.

Catmate was both an indoors and outdoors cat, but always indoors at night. Then one evening, when he was about three years of age, I could not find him anywhere in the house. He was nowhere to be found. I went outside calling out to him over and over, and shaking his dry food box — shake, shake, shake — which was always a sure way of rounding him up, but all to no avail. It was getting quite late and wherever was Catmate? I remember the date so well: it was Boxing Day 1997, and in the traditional Australian way, after all the festivities and fun of Christmas Day, I was relaxing at home with my sister Jan, who was staying with me. Catmate and my other gorgeous cat, a beautiful black, long-haired, gentle female named Shadow, had both shared in Christmas Day festivities and both cats had been dressed up with a red ribbon around their collars. Now here in the dark of the next night Catmate had gone missing. I had an awful sense of dread.

Finally, at around midnight, Jan and I decided to go searching for Catmate by driving around the local area. We had only gone about halfway down the hill when out of the still night air I heard the most plaintive of sounds: a sad, desperate, pleading 'meeeooow, meeeooow'. And then I saw Catmate. All I could see was his face and the front part of his head, stuck fast in the narrow exit of a stormwater drain. Jan and I rushed to help and to comfort him, and realised he could not move forwards or backwards. We also quickly realised that we could do nothing ourselves to release him from this frightening situation.

I left Jan in charge to comfort Catmate, rushed up the hill on foot, raced indoors and rang for emergency help. I was feeling fairly desperate, and quickly explained the circumstances. Thankfully help was swift in arriving as two men from the local fire brigade turned up within about fifteen minutes. They removed the large, heavy manhole cover by levering it up and out of position, and one of them then climbed down into the stormwater drain, where poor Catmate was literally dangling down, his hind legs stretched into the hole below.

It was distressing to see Catmate in such a position. He was obviously caught so tightly and no doubt painfully, and his distressed cries as he was being rescued turned to helpless yowling. One of the men gradually levered him down, hind legs first, to free him. At last his poor little head and face appeared backwards through the manhole and there he was, back with me, and with his little red Christmas ribbon still around his collar — after all that! Jan and I expressed our gratitude to Catmate's kind and calm rescuers, and we wrapped Catmate in a towel, took him up the hill and then safely indoors for the night. Home at last! The ordeal was thankfully over and Catmate was none the worse for wear. After eating a little snack he settled down happily for the night. He was such an inspiring little fellow, just ready to get on with life.

I am pleased to say that Catmate never did get into such a dire scrape or misadventure again, but it certainly did not stop his sense of adventure, exploration and just plain fun. I wrote soon after to the Commissioner of Fire Brigades in New South Wales, expressing my gratitude for the help of those two men who saved my treasured cat from a situation he could not have escaped from on his own. I received a very kind letter of reply from the Commissioner. It is indeed a blessing to live in the sort of community where such help for rescue is so readily available.

It was only recently, in April 2011, that my beautiful golden feline friend went to his final rest and I am deeply grieving the loss of my beautiful little boy. Farewelling him was one of the saddest and the most heartbreaking times in my life. It was very humbling, a gracious gift and a privilege indeed to have had such a special and deep friendship and communication with such a wonderful creature. He has left his spirit of wonderful love and loyalty deeply within me, for which I am immeasurably grateful. He will always have a very special, very endearing and very enduring presence in my heart. It could not be otherwise.

Those of us who are blessed to share our lives with feline company know only too well how our charming little companions can amuse and surprise us — and often when we least expect it.

This story is about Catmate, who got up to unimagined antics one day while watching television. Well, I was watching television but I didn't really think that he was watching it too, when suddenly he made it quite clear how he felt about what he saw. It was a gardening and nature type show and there on the screen was a featured report on a native Australian bird — a beautiful sulphur-crested cockatoo — and this bird was clearly on Catmate's territory. From his comfortable sitting position, Catmate stood up and strode towards the television. He settled down resolutely and stared at the screen, transfixed and determined. I was amused and amazed. Next thing, loudly and clearly, he hissed at the bird on the screen, then stood up, turned around, hissed across the room, then hissed to both sides, and having dignified the occasion in stunning feline fashion he stalked off in disgust to another part of the room. He then settled down to ignore the whole upsetting episode and sleep it off.

Shadow also caught the television viewing bug — perhaps Catmate taught her this. This sharing of television viewing time was an instance of how Shadow and Catmate chose to spend their time together; a very loving feline bond had developed between them and they used to look out for one another, with a strong awareness of each other. Over the years they discovered plenty of together nooks, including, of course, sleeping on my bed at night. So it was really quite natural that they would watch television together too. Their greater tuning-in, however, was in their awareness of and communication with one another, which I found truly captivating and wondrous.

Shadow was such a beautiful cat, a shy little individual and very timid, a quiet and loving friend. She had long, soft fur and gorgeous yellow–green eyes which shone like beacons in the night. To receive the love and trust of such a precious little soul was a gift indeed. We spent many happy years together. Shadow blessed my life from the time she was about two years of age, when as a sad, lost, forlorn and bedraggled stray cat she was looking for a loving home, which she found with my mother, who adored cats. That was back in 1991, and Mum named her Shadow because of the delightful way she used to walk along near her, keeping Mum company like a little shadow. Mum loved Shadow so much. I spent a fair amount of time at my mother's home, so naturally I got to know Shadow very well and love her too.

I moved back into the house with my mother in 1993, and when in 1996 Mum went into a nursing home Shadow came totally into my care. By that time another wonderful cat, my gorgeous boy Catmate, had also come to share in our lives, so Shadow had a special feline friend. Luckily Mum did have some occasional day trips home and would spend some time with both Shadow and Catmate on these occasions, before very sadly Mum passed away in the middle of 1998.

I never wanted to think of the day that Shadow and I would part, could not even start to imagine such a time, but it was around the time she was seventeen years of age that I sensed her days were coming to an end. It was not long after Christmas 2006 when I had to admit to myself that my darling little girl was going downhill. Shadow was a very brave little soul and had needed a lot of very careful treatment and veterinary observation for diabetes for over three years at the stage when she started to show undeniable decline. She had been looked after by two vets in a local practice, so I naturally sought their assistance now — she had certainly lost her appetite and had become very lethargic, and was losing weight. The vets explained she had a liver condition and helped me to accept that there was nothing more that could be done to help Shadow improve medically.

Shadow and Catmate had bonded over the years, having spent over eleven years together, so losing Shadow was also going to be so very hard for poor Catmate. Both cats used to sleep on my bed at night, were affectionate companions to one another and enjoyed just being near one another. They were a great pair together.

I felt overcome by a mountain of despair and helpless grief in those weeks watching Shadow decline and seeking help for her. I shed so many tears in my heartache. During those difficult weeks I relied heavily on the advice of the two vets. They were both very compassionate and honest in their advice to me and in answer to my questions. It was so hard to face the truth, so very hard, but I came to realise that euthanasia was far the best choice for darling Shadow. One of my friends, a pet carer, supported me enormously over those weeks and understood the situation I was facing. In addition, my friend put me in touch with a wonderful minister of the Uniting Church, himself an animal lover and sensitive to the needs of animals and those caring for them. I also learned that this minister held special services for 'Blessing of the animals' around the time of Saint Francis of Assisi Day in the grounds of his church. I approached him to see whether he would be present when Shadow was put to sleep at home, and he was just so obliging. I think he was a bit surprised too, as he had not been called upon for this particular pastoral service before but was more than willing to help.

The minister arrived at my home with thoughtful and special prayers. The vet then arrived with his vet nurse, and my pet carer friend also arrived. Shadow and I were surrounded by so much love and care. My friend read a beautiful poem about a pet, which the minister had brought along with him. I then picked up my precious Shadow for the very last time and carried her over near Catmate so they could say their farewells in their own feline way. I am sure Catmate realised Shadow was about to leave us, animals being so extraordinarily perceptive. The vet then eased Shadow into eternal sleep and she slipped away as I sat their cradling her. I could not bring myself to look down at Shadow at first, but when I did I could see that her suffering was clearly over.

I had previously arranged for a pet cremation service to call afterwards, and a caring young man soon arrived. He waited patiently, and after a short time I stood up and carried Shadow's still little body accompanied by her blanket outside and into the vehicle, and placed two of her toys in there too. I chose to have Shadow's ashes returned to me in a wooden box with an engraved plaque and a photograph of her placed on top. I look at the photograph of her so often, which shows her in her heyday up in the jacaranda tree. Somehow I know that she is in a better place now, and totally safe and at peace, and I have such special and wonderful memories of her and the ways she blessed my life.

Animals feel grief too, and I sensed it was a hard and strange time for Catmate. Catmate had lost a wonderful friend, just as I had.

Several months later I held a memorial service in celebration of Shadow's wonderful life, conducted by the minister and attended by a gathering of a few friends, including my pet carer friend. I gave a little talk about Shadow, recalling some events in her life as a celebration of all she had meant to my mother and to me.

It is so very hard to say goodbye to whomever we hold dear, and such was the case with Shadow. It seemed that those years with Shadow had passed so quickly. Time spent with our treasured pet companions is so precious; they are such loving and trusted friends who bless our lives immeasurably. I will always be grateful for the memories of my precious years with Shadow, whose spirit of love and trust remains with me forever.

CRYSTAL

Paige Foley-Dunn

Crystal is a cat who lives on the street where I work. We met around three years ago, shortly after I started working there. At first I'd say hello every now and then and have a pat as I normally would with any friendly feline. After a while she seemed to be out waiting for me and I would look forward to seeing her before and after work each day.

Most days when I arrive I can see the silhouette of a tiny cat up the street; she'll spot me and come galloping towards me, light footed and happy to see me. Some days she'll see me first and come from around the back of the house or from under a parked car, meowing as she arrives. Other days she'll hide and just as I get close she'll jump out of a well-positioned tree and startle me — I'm sure if cats could show us they were laughing she'd be doubled over with laughter after giving me a fright.

In winter we brave the rain just for a quick catch-up. I ask her what she's been up to and she meows to fill me in. And sometimes when it's summer I just let her be while she sleeps in a patch of sun. Spring is another thing; there is a family of wattle birds who live and nest nearby, and we get swooped on from every direction. I run up the street with my hands over my head and when I look down there's Crystal running beside me ... just for fun.

The *Oxford English Dictionary* says 'a friend is someone whom one knows and with whom one has a bond of mutual affection'. Animal lovers know this, I know this, I think Crystal knows this. We're friends.

Crystal

THE ADVENTURES OF MINNIE AND LUNA

Zoë Dunn, aged 11

We got our cats, Minnie Minerva McGonagall and Lightning Luna Lovegood, from the Cat Protection Society about three years ago. I was over the moon when we took them home. They were so tiny and so cute. I couldn't wait till we got home so they could have fun at our house. They settled in immediately, however we found that Minnie Min was terrified of my dad, James, and strangers, but mostly men. My mum thinks that maybe she had been scared by a big man before she was rescued by the CPS.

The things I love about my cats are the way they play — they are just so cute together. They snuggle up together in winter for warmth and look as if they are hugging. When Phoebe, my sister, or I sleep in, Mum sends the cats marching into our room to wake us up. They wake us up with their snuggles, their sniffs and their purrs. We call this the Cat Alarm.

They are not always so good. Once we came home and smelled cat food. We were confused until ... we saw ripped open sachets of cat food *all* over the house. My mum had not closed the lid of the cat food box properly and the naughty cats had prised it open and had a feast. Mum even found a few opened sachets under our bed! Now mum always closes the lid well. But Luna still tries her luck by sitting there and having a big old scratch at the plastic box, hoping for another lucky chance to get it open. When Mum buys the box of cat food, Luna sometimes tries to rip it open when we are not around. She tears off strips of cardboard but so far she has never succeeded. Both Minnie and Luna always get into the clean washing and have a little nap — always before we get a chance to fold it! Sometimes they decide to have a fight: they wrestle and then chase each other all over the house, leaping from chair to chair.

Having Luna and Minnie has changed my life because they brighten up my day and when I am sad or crying they come in and comfort me. This is why our two cats are so important and are the cutest cats in the universe.

MINNIE AND THE HORRID BIRDBATH ADVENTURE AND HER SAVIOUR, LUNA!

Phoebe Dunn, aged 9

One day around a year ago lived two of the cutest cats in our galaxy, Minnie Minerva McGonagall, otherwise known as Minnie or Min Min, and Lightning Luna Lovegood, otherwise known as Luna or Luna Buna.

One sunny, clear day, my kind mother Catherine had decided to let the cute cats have a run around in the small, green garden. Minnie and Luna loved their time in the garden. Mum, my sister Zoë, my aunty Janie and I had gone to the movies.

The cats were playing outside when Minnie leapt next door and landed on an unsteady birdbath. Since the birdbath was not connected bottom to top, when Min Min landed on it the birdbath flipped on top of her. Soon Luna discovered the collapsed bird bath and heard a faint 'meow' so Luna Buna stood by the dirty birdbath, waiting for Min Min to be rescued.

After we arrived home, my mum received a phone call from our very friendly next door neighbour, Fay, who said, 'Sorry to bother you but I thought I should tell you that my old, smelly, dirty birdbath fell on your cat Min Min.' Fay said she only knew something was wrong because Luna was sitting next to the fallen birdbath and would not move. Mum went outside and saw the saviour Luna and the smelly Minnie.

So immediately after, Mum had the dirty deed of giving Minnie a bath. This was not so easy. Minnie was covered in green slime, mud, leaves and twigs. Mum had to get into the bath with her to get all the yucky gunk off Minnie. Minnie was not happy. She never wanted to go outside again. Now Minnie and Luna are very happy indoors!

BADCAT

Ellen McGinness

Four years ago we discovered a very angry cat in our garden. We already had three cats of our own who did not take kindly to this visitor. Badcat was the nickname we gave him as he would spray and defecate in our house and hide under beds and come lunging out to attack us. I letterbox dropped the street, asking if he belonged to anyone. Eventually I discovered he lived three doors down.

Badcat remained a nuisance but we learned to live with it. Early one morning I was stirred from sleep by a loud purr, marching on my body and a wet patch on my stomach. I thought it was my cat Spuddy. To my surprise, it was Badcat. He was so needy and soft I couldn't believe it. From that moment on we bonded.

He had been living with us on-again, off-again for four years and eventually he never left our house (our cats were very disappointed). Badcat was so in love with us he would leap onto our shoulders, drool into our laps and constantly cry if he was locked out. He became a part of the family. We had always thought Badcat was neglected or unloved so he got special treats, nightly dinners and his own water bowl to play with (he loves playing with water). Badcat also slept with me every night squeezed in with two human bodies and two other felines. He would leave a wet patch where he drooled.

We thought he was so starved of love because he showed so much need for it. One Saturday morning I noticed he had blood coming from his mouth and decided it was time to talk to his owners. I took him down in our cat carrier, not sure if they really loved him and would take him to the vet. The owners were lovely! Boy, had I got it wrong. They took him to the vet and it was a minor allergy. We talked a lot over that day and I found out they were cat lovers too and had a big white inside cat.

I found out from his owners that Badcat was nine years old and they'd had him for seven years. He was a rescue cat who had had bad luck with his previous homes. The owner said that he never really seemed to be happy with them and was shocked when he found out that Badcat was so affectionate to us. It just goes to show that cats truly pick their owners. Compared to his own home, ours seems a lot less appealing. But to him, he has found love. We may not have the giant scratch towers, the wonderful catnip products and gourmet meals but that did not stop him from setting up residence. Badcat's owners said we could adopt him as he seemed to like us more than them.

When I move out of my family home and have to leave my cats (our cats) with my parents, I will take Badcat with me. My cats can't stand him so they will be happy to have him gone. Until then, we will love him and feed him and I will never stop cuddling him.

FELIX AND LILY

Nikki D'Silva

When Chanel from the Cat Protection Society asked me to write a small article for the society's book I was flattered and happy to share the story of Felix and Lily, my two adopted cats. To be honest I am not sure exactly how Felix and Lily started their lives, but they were discovered in an alley, along with their four other brother and sisters, by a good Samaritan who then brought them into the Cat Protection Society for care.

Felix and Lily are not like most of the kittens brought into the shelter. They are white, fluffy and have blue and green eyes (well, Felix has one blue and one green, and Lily has two blue). There is also one other thing that is very special about my little ones: Lily is completely deaf.

Generally, when I tell people that Lily is deaf their first reaction is pity for her, and then they feel sad, but I tell them not to worry or to be sad because she doesn't care that she can't hear and has a great life. To be honest, when I went to adopt Felix and Lily I had to think long and hard about what it would mean to have a 'special needs' cat, but after a cuddle I really had no choice but to adopt them.

Within the litter of six, two of the kittens were deaf, but from the way they played and interacted with each other you wouldn't know. When I adopted Lily, the staff at the shelter explained that I also needed to adopt one of the hearing kittens so that they could help support the deaf kitten; that was not a problem for me, as I wanted to adopt two so they would have company during the day while I was at work.

So when I brought my two new babies home I knew they would develop a special bond, and they certainly have. Felix (my hearing cat) has always looked after Lily. If I come home and Lily is still asleep, Felix will go and wake her to make sure she doesn't

Felix and Lily

miss out. If I am putting their dinner together and she is in another room, he will run to go and get her. He is always taking care of her.

The bond they have is really sweet to watch. They have their disagreements like any brother and sister, but for the most part they are loving siblings. They sleep together, eat together and play together. While Felix looks after Lily because she can't hear, Lily looks after Felix when things get a little scary, for as protective as Felix is he's also a bit of a scaredy cat. So when people come around to visit, Felix lets Lily know something is different in the house then hides under my bed, and Lily keeps the visitor busy so they don't go looking for Felix.

If you are thinking about adopting a cat with a 'special need' and are concerned about what it will mean for you and your family, all I can say is, don't be afraid — they will bring you joy, love and appreciation because they know they are special and love you for loving them. The only difference I have noticed between having a deaf cat and a hearing cat is that I have to make eye contact with Lily to get her attention instead of calling out to her, and that's it.

I love the two new additions to my family and wouldn't change a thing. Thank you to the Cat Protection Society for saving them in the first place, and thank you for letting me adopt them; they certainly have found a loving, caring home.

THE STORY OF
SATCHMO AND MONTY

Brad and Sarah

Satchmo was adopted by my partner, Sarah, five years ago from the CPS and moved into a home full of furry friends (three cats and a dog at this time). Included in his furry family list was a grand old lady Labrador called Chloe, and the friendship between Satchmo and Chloe included lots of mutual cleaning and Satchmo finishing the dog food whenever possible. Satchmo's best mate was Battlecat, with whom he had formed a very close bond, and as a kitten he learned all a cat needs to know from Battlecat.

On a very unfortunate day as we were returning from holidaying in Queensland, Battlecat was killed by a car while crossing the road. This was a terrible event as the cats were extremely close and Battlecat was a very special fellow. His loss is still very much mourned by his human mum (Sarah). Not long after, Sarah and I decided to move in together. I had been thinking for some time of getting a cat myself. So Sarah and I went to CPS to see what kittens and cats they had. We had a look through the kittens and none of them really took our fancy, so we had a look at the cats to see if there was anything there. While looking around we occasionally saw a flash of white as a white kitten bolted about stealing toys and running under the cat cages with them. We had met Monty.

So Sarah and I thought about Monty, weighed up the pros and cons and eventually went back to pick him up a couple of days later.

It would still be another week or two before we moved

Monty and Satchmo

into our new place, which meant that Monty and I would spend a week together in a *very* small studio apartment, in a holding pattern you could say. It was as if a little white hurricane had struck my tiny apartment! This quiet but active kitten turned into a very vocal and hyperactive white devil who would tear around for ten minutes then sleep for five minutes. Night-time consisted of me being stalked while I slept followed by fun in the kitty litter, only for the cycle to be repeated again and again. Obviously I couldn't wait to move.

Sarah and I found a large apartment that suited our requirements and would also give the soon-to-be furry flatmates enough room and windows for stimulation. We went out and bought cat towers (including scratching posts), another scratching post, plus some toys and treats. We moved everything in. Then came the time to move in the furry flatmates. Monty was first in as he was only around the corner; then came Satchmo's turn. Sarah and I were pretty excited about this and made what we soon found out to be a 'rookie' mistake. Monty had already been gallivanting about the apartment for a couple of hours, so once we brought Satchmo into the apartment it already smelled like Monty. So Satchmo hid in the bedroom under the bed for two days ... Bad start.

After two days and some coaching from Sarah and I, Satchmo started to investigate the apartment and avoided his new flatmate. Thankfully, after a couple of weeks they started to play and mostly enjoy each other's company. In no time at all they were play-fighting to own the top of the tower and the prime location in front of the heater.

We can say now that they are very good friends. They spend all their time together and have regular 'rumbles' to sort out who is the alpha cat (mostly the white devil until he takes it too far and earns a smack-down). It's great to see that from such an inauspicious start they have become so close.

Thanks CPS for all your help.

SCHIELE KENNEDY

Laura and Jason Kennedy

When we went to the Cat Protection Society in July 2008 we were looking for a companion for our nine-month-old kitten, Klimt. It was breaking our hearts every time we left the house to leave our indoor cat all alone and we wanted to get her a kitty friend. After the agonising process of walking into the CPS and only being able to take one cat home we selected another nine-month-old kitten (called Milko at the time) that we promptly named Schiele in the hopes that he and Klimt would be great friends.

When we first got Schiele home we set him up with a safe room so he could settle in without being pestered by the queen of the house. He promptly ran under a cabinet and remained there for a few hours. After a few human visits and encouraging whispers Schiele started to wander out from his hiding spot. He crept slowly at first and then charged from under the cabinet, delivering a forceful head butt followed by a tremendous flop onto the carpet with bundles of purring. He had officially stolen my heart.

Within no time Klimt and Schiele were quite inseparable yet they are complete opposites in almost every way. While Klimt is fiery and often terrifyingly intelligent, Schiele is adorably gentle and often appears to have absolutely no idea what he is doing. In the face of the dangerous unknown he is all flight while she is all fight. He is the floppy to her stroppy.

One of Schiele's stranger habits is to pull people towards his favourite stretch of carpet in the house, that we have since named the Schiele Field. When you go to get out of bed in the morning or are simply pottering about in the kitchen he is often at your feet looking up at you. As you then go to stroke him he meows and scrambles a few paces forward, waits, meows again; you then walk towards him and this pattern repeats until he has secured your presence in the Field. There he flops with an almighty thud onto the carpet and purrs madly while accepting belly rubs.

The Field is in the living room about 2 metres from our couch, towards our front door. When we are on the couch and Klimt wants affection she simply jumps up and picks a lap to curl up on, as most logical creatures would do. Schiele, meanwhile, squats firmly in the Field and meows at various intervals until someone gets up and gives him affection. He glares at you, seemingly confused, wondering why you haven't got up and come over to him yet. Even if you sweep him up and bring him over to the couch he will still run back to the Field and wait for your return.

As far as we can tell there is nothing particularly special about this stretch of carpet and though these nutty little patterns happen regularly, they don't last for any sort of concerning duration. He is not obsessive, just particular. If you don't comply with his requests he soon finds somewhere cosy to sleep or finds a suitable perch near a window to do some bird watching.

Schiele has made the perfect addition to our family. We will be forever grateful to the CPS for rescuing him and allowing this divine little being into our lives.

KATIE LEARNS TO CLIMB

Grace Tam and Darryn Rogers

I adopted Katie and Lily in 2009 when they were six-month-old kittens. They bring me a lot of joy and laughter.

Katie and Lily are sisters. Lily is a hunter and loves to climb trees. Katie is the complete opposite. She's a lover and is usually found by the window peacefully watching the world go by. Lily's fearless personality meant she quickly learned to master her natural agility. She can jump up onto a desk, washing machine or piano without making a noise. Katie's timid personality meant it took her more time to master her physical coordination. She is much better at finding the best secret hiding places around the house.

Katie is observant. After watching Lily jump up gracefully onto the piano she decided to have a try. She sat in front of the piano, carefully measuring the distance and height, taking her time. She carefully calculated the amount of energy needed. She launched towards the piano and ... thud, she hit her head on the keyboard and flopped to the floor.

One day, I found Katie and Lily at the bottom of a tree, eyeing the first branch. Lily launched onto the trunk and with two swift moves she climbed up to the first branch. Katie also launched onto the trunk. She stretched as high as she could on her tippy toes, excitedly scratching the

Lily and Katie

highest part of the trunk that she could reach without taking her back legs off the ground.

To help Katie improve her physical coordination and to add more variety to their games, I invested in a funky cat tree — custom made, 2 metres tall, with a hollow in the trunk and platforms for sitting on. I wave a feather at the top platform of the tree and Lily jumps from platform to platform to reach the feather. Clever Lily soon worked out various paths to the top — in the hollow, out onto the first platform, then in the hollow again, onto the second platform and then up the side of the carpeted tree trunk to the top platform. Katie is a bit more careful ... into the hollow and out to the first platform ... stop ... measure ... into the hollow and out onto the second platform ... to the third platform ... to the top ... But when she arrives she discovers Lily is there. Lily declares her territory with a claw in the air, and Katie retreats.

I went out to look for Katie and Lily one lazy Saturday afternoon. 'Katie! Lily!' I called. No answer. Then I spotted a black cat stuck halfway up the side of a tree, clinging desperately onto the trunk ... that was Katie. Lily was happily sitting on the first branch staring at me as if to say, 'Look how high I am!'

One day Katie will make it to that first branch. I'm sure.

MY LIFE WITH CHILDREN
AND CATS

Samantha Kelly

For many years as a veterinary nurse and working at Cat Protection Society, I educated people on how to introduce their cat/s to their new baby or the introduction of a kitten or cat to an existing family with children. I used this information when I introduced my two cats to my son and then my daughter.

Nothing could prepare me for the love I felt watching my cats interact with my children. It all started when my son Ethan was in my womb. He was a very active baby, always kicking. My shy cat Lexy has always liked to be cuddled by me and lie on my lap. She used my baby 'bump' as a head rest. Ethan would kick her in the head and she never seemed to care. It was amusing to watch and I wondered if she knew something was different.

When I brought my son home from the hospital he was in the lounge room, sleeping in the portable car capsule. My other cat Saffy came over to say hello to me. My son made a sound as she walked past his capsule and the look on her face was priceless. If she could speak our language she would have said, 'What is this thing and why is it here? I hope it is not staying!' However, once she got used to the sounds that a baby makes she used to love lying on the same pillow that I had Ethan on while I was feeding him. Her purring was very soothing for my son and me. It was a magical time.

Saffy did the same thing when I had my daughter, Ashlyn. The cats used to also enjoy watching the children on the play mat. It seemed that they knew a baby couldn't move much unless I picked them up so it was safe. It is so adorable when your child notices a cat for the first time. At first there is confusion then a smile of sheer delight at this moving 'toy'. Every time one of our cats would enter the room, a smile would start across the baby's face, followed a squeal of delight (which the cats didn't like).

Once both the children started crawling the cats were not so keen as these babies then moved towards them. It was unrequited love at this stage. The kids loved the cats but the feeling wasn't always mutual. It was funny, however, watching the cats see my son or daughter crawling down the hall towards them; the cats would wait to the last possible moment to move. When the kids became toddlers this was the hardest time. They started to walk, which was confusing for the cats as they must have thought, 'How is this possible?' As any parent knows, toddlers are very loud and active, a combination that not all cats like. However, you can supervise and teach your child to always be gentle and to leave the cat alone if they move away and want to be left alone. My children have also been taught never to disturb cats when sleeping, eating or using the litter tray. Once your child learns how to be quieter around the cat and not be so excitable, a special bond develops.

My son Ethan is now five years old. He has always been pretty gentle with both cats. He won over Saffy first (she is the more confident cat). She enjoys being petted by him and purrs very loudly for him. I told him if he sits quietly with her then she will happily stay there. He is so proud that he has won her over. Saffy also 'talks' to him, something she usually reserves for my husband and me. I explained to my son that this is her special communication with people she loves and trusts. It is a mutually satisfying experience for both of them. Lexy will also allow him to pet her if she is in the mood. She is a shy cat and has always been that way. I find as my son grows up she is treating him differently and likes him more the older he gets.

Ethan and Lexy

Ashlyn is two-and-a-half years old. She is a very independent toddler but has now started to calm down and does not get so excited when she sees the cats. Saffy now allows Ashlyn to pat and cuddle her and it makes my daughter extremely happy. Lexy will stay in the same room as my daughter as long as she is not running into the room or lunging towards Lexy. It makes me want to cry with sheer joy when she says, 'Saffy/Lexy loves me' or 'I love Lexy and Saffy', as does seeing the smile on my son's face when he is petting or cuddling Saffy and telling me how much they love each other. He feels extra special if Lexy allows him to give her a pat, too.

I can see the love my cats bring to my children and how much they love all animals as a result of being brought up with pets. My cats are also benefiting from the experience as now they get more attention and more pats. It is important for children to grow up with animals as it teaches them to respect, care for and be kind to them.

CUSTARD

Lisa Rowland

When Phil and I first met, Phil had a beautiful dog, Paddy, and I had two gorgeous cats, Billy and Lou-Lou. After fourteen years together we lost all our babies in a short space of time. We were devastated. Our lives had revolved around them.

About two years later with so much love to give, we decided to look at adopting another pet. So we thought, 'The Cat Protection Society is just at the top of our street, let's go see who we might meet.' It was a Friday afternoon. We met Custard first. She was a real cranky pants and wouldn't let us touch her. We met so many other beautiful cats, some affectionate, some aloof, but something drew us back to Custard. She didn't seem interested in the other cats. She was playful with her toys and active, but a little insular. We went home to think. The next day Phil had to work so he told me I could decide. Secretly, I had already decided it was going to be Custard.

My sister, Karen, came with me on Saturday morning. I couldn't wait, though when we got to the CPS I wasn't game to pick up Custard because I knew she was feisty. So one of the staff put her in her cage, we covered her up and Karen carried her home. Once home, we opened the cage and out Custard jumped; she had a look around and then was straight up

Custard

on the couch for a reassuring scratch under the chin. Once Custard had established that there was food to be had, she was sold. It took a little while for Custard to warm to us. She was a bit stand-offish at first but we were patient with her and let her find her own way in her own time.

Custard has now come to love and trust us, and she is settled and happy. We have recently celebrated the first anniversary of welcoming her into our family. The things she loves the most are food, first and foremost, hunting lizards in the backyard, snoozing on her plush cushions and watching telly with us. She especially loves shows about sharks, although I did catch her watching *Prisoner* recently.

The Cat Protection Society was fantastic to deal with. All the staff there are wonderful and kind people and we thank them for introducing us to our special girl, Custard.

MOGS AND BISCUIT ET AL.

Kristina Vesk

I became fascinated with Siamese cats as a small child when we visited friends of my parents who had one of these exotic creatures. I had lived with cats — moggies — all my life, and loved them, but there was something about Siamese that captured my imagination. It was not until I was in my twenties that one came into my life. She had been surrendered to a vet clinic in sad circumstances and my friend, who was the vet, knew I was looking for a cat. She made so much noise during the hour-long trip home it was almost tempting to turn around. The Siamese yowl gets under your skin like a baby's cry; it cannot be ignored.

Her amazing relationship with us took off about ten to fifteen minutes after arriving home. She checked us and the home thoroughly. It wasn't what she was used to; we lived in a tiny inner-west terrace, whereas she'd come from a big semi-rural property, but she seemed to like it. Her real passion, though, was not for her surroundings but for company and conversation. If we had a party she would circulate, going from group to group and joining in with a word here and there (and if she thought no one was looking, a surreptitious lap from a wine glass). She would go visiting with us, now enjoying car trips sitting on my lap on the passenger side, watching out of the closed window, often causing a double-take from passing motorists. Dogs love car trips, but cats? Well, Mogs adored going wherever we did, making herself immediately at home in other people's houses.

Unfortunately Mogs also liked to explore the neighbourhood and as she never went out to the busy front street but only around the back lanes, I thought she was safe. One day she brought home with her a little calico friend, who stayed at a safe distance from us on the roof. Mogs tried to entice her inside, this was obvious, but the little tortie and white girl we saw was very clearly a wary street cat. We put food out for her (which Mogs politely would not eat) and over time she gradually moved in closer. Finally we trapped her and had her desexed.

Mrs Biscuit, as she became known, forgave us this intrusion but continued to venture in only just near the back door; yet she desperately adored Mogs and worked on overcoming her fear of us in order to spend time with her precious friend. The months went by and everyone was happy; Mrs Biscuit loved Mogs but did not feel the need to love us, and that was okay.

One day, Mogs disappeared. We were distraught and set up search parties, put up posters, put ads in the paper. She had a collar and tag, and a microchip (this was in the mid 1980s, long before they were common); surely we would find her. Mrs Biscuit would turn up in the back courtyard, looking at us with big concerned eyes. Where is my friend? She joined us in crying. Incredibly, she even joined us on the bed — something she had never done. I think she was there in the hope that if her beloved friend came home, she would be there, waiting.

It was about two weeks later that we discovered the horrific truth: Mogs had been killed by a car and the council had literally thrown her away with the garbage, ignoring her collar and tag, showing contempt for her and the people (and cat) who loved her so much. We wailed with grief at home that night, and Mrs Biscuit sat there with us. She realised that our hope was lost and she knew what this meant. Two mornings later we found her dead on our doorstep; the neighbour said she'd been run over on the main road, a place she never went. I think she just could not live without the love of her best friend.

We couldn't live there anymore — there was too much grief and too many painful memories. I swore I would never again let a cat of mine go outdoors. We moved into a unit in the Eastern Suburbs and life continued. I missed feline company but I was still quite fragile. On my birthday I was taken out for a 'surprise' — it was to the home of a breeder of Siamese cats! She was a lovely woman and very fussy about who adopted her kittens. She lived in a large villa-style unit and her cats ranged about freely (indoors only), in good health and in good spirits. I'd never seen a Siamese kitten before — their points are so pale they are almost invisible. One particular kitten made a political point by batting at some character on a news program and I liked her style. After many words of advice from the breeder and an insistence I have the kitten desexed by six months of age (early desexing was uncommon at this time), the tiny, pale creature came home with us.

Time went on and Lydia's points became dark and her nose grew longer and her face more angular; she was wonderful company but I always felt a bit sad about leaving her alone during the day. A newspaper ad caught my eye one day: Devon Rex kittens. I'd never seen a Devon Rex in person, as it were, so went 'just to look'. In contrast to the wonderful registered breeder from whom we got Lydia, this person ... well, she said: 'She's a bit inbred so if she dies in the next fourteen days you'll get your money back.' I was so horrified I just had to get the kitten out of there.

This gorgeous little alien-looking creature was so friendly she and Lydia became instant pals. Two weeks passed and our little Rex was still alive! She was desexed when older and all her vet checks were fine.

While Lydia was quite refined and well mannered, Tati (named after French comic Jacques Tati) was cheeky and wild. She would hide on top of the fridge and launch herself onto the shoulders of unsuspecting visitors. Lydia would sit and watch the episode, a Mona Lisa smile on her beautiful face. The two girls would play together, eat together, sleep together. They adored each other and they adored us; we adored them.

I was pregnant and as we lived in a small unit the baby's cot was going to be in our room. We installed a screen door on the room so when the time came at least the cats could still see into the room if not sleep in it. Until then it was 'access all areas' and the cats slept on my growing belly each night. Lydia was curled up on me when I went into labour; she was a little miffed when she had to get up so I could go to hospital.

They dealt amazingly well with the new arrival and being locked out from the big bed was made up for by the presence of a cosy pram in the corridor. There was still enough room on my lap for two cats while I nursed my new baby. Later, teething rings would be stolen for toys. Teddies were good for snuggling. Well before the year's end, the screen door was off and there were three people, two cats and numerous teddies all sharing one bedroom!

One Sunday morning I heard a horrible sound coming from the bathroom and ran in to find Tati curled up and fitting on the floor. My husband rushed her to the vet; on the way her heart stopped beating but the vet had a defibrillator which he applied to her tiny body. Alas it was no use. She died from congenital heart failure. She had lived for only a year.

Here we were again in mourning but we had our jobs and our baby to distract us. Lydia sunk into a deep, deep depression. She showed no interest in games, she stopped purring and she barely ate. She was inconsolable and I thought the only thing to do was to distract her utterly with a new friend. For the first two weeks, she treated Imogen (a pretty Tonkinese) like an unwelcome intruder and yet she was careful about it, for Imogen was only ten weeks old.

I can't remember exactly but it took less than a month before Lydia and Imogen were firm friends. Meanwhile, this young kitten identified strongly with the human 'kitten' and sought to copy her and be with her. It was quite hilarious to watch them; Imogen loved to curl up on newspaper so Julia (the baby) would do the same. Imogen stole the smaller of Julia's stacking rings to play with. Lydia would perch high on a table or shelf — safely away from tiny hands — while Imogen and Julia played together with blocks or playdough. Imogen and Julia were like sisters and Lydia and I were the mums.

The years only served to strengthen the bonds. We moved house, Julia started school, I changed jobs. When I separated from my husband, the cats came to stay with us at my mother's. Later Julia and I moved into the house next door but now Lydia and Imogen enjoyed living with someone who was home all day, which was a good thing since a tiny five-week-old tabby was dumped in our street and needed a home. Some months later, I adopted a little black and white sister, Lucy, for Top Cat, the tabby. They lived in our house, and Lydia and Imogen lived next door with my mum. While Lydia and Imogen were devoted to each other like some legendary couple, Top Cat and Lucy's relationship was more Bobby and Cindy Brady — not exactly affectionate but a recognition that family comes first.

At about thirteen years, Lydia developed arthritis but the vet prescribed injections that put the spring back in her paws. Imogen was still chasing the pink stacking ring from Julia's baby toys when Julia was doing her school certificate. During the day, the girls slept together in their basket or one on each side of the heater if it was on. There were competitions for who could be closest to my mother's face when they sat one on top of the other on her lap. Imogen usually won, placing victorious paws one on each of my mother's shoulders.

At the beginning of 2010, Lydia was diagnosed with early stage renal failure. As Imogen was now also quite old, both cats were put on a special diet for this, though Imogen showed no clinical signs of the disease. Their health was stable until, in July, Imogen suddenly fell ill and lost a lot of weight in a matter of days. She was diagnosed with end-stage renal failure. A couple of nights on fluids at the vet would tell us whether she had months or days left to live. Lydia waited patiently at home for her sister to return, and when Imogen came home with a healthy appetite thanks to the fluid therapy, we were all relieved. However, within 36 hours she was worse, at which point Lydia stopped eating. The vet was consulted. There

Top Cat

was no quality of life for Imogen to be left at the vets on fluid therapy. Lydia had been checked the previous week; she should be okay.

Within days, each had reached practically the same point in renal failure — a clear determination on Lydia's part to go with her sister. They were put to sleep at home, Lydia in my arms, Imogen in Julia's. We wrapped them in bunny rugs my grandmother had sewn for Julia when she was a baby. They were cremated together and their ashes are at home, and they are at peace.

Julia had just finished her trial exams for her final high school examinations. We went away for a few days and my mother had to mind Top Cat and Lucy. She missed her little Oriental girls so much and was quietly grieving when Top Cat came up to her and stared. He had never been given to affection (most likely his traumatic past) but now he stared intently at my mother's lap. He leapt into it and then looked horrified at what he had done, something so alien to him. He jumped off. But then he came back and, almost as though gritting his teeth, jumped up again and this time reached and put his paws up, one on each of my mother's shoulders. He held the pose for a moment, looking into her eyes, and then she cried and he hopped off. I can only believe this was Imogen, letting my mother know that she was okay; it was a final farewell.

. Top Cat has never done such a thing again, though he continues to work on his relationship skills.

CARING FOR CATS

Dr Anne Fawcett

BA(Hons) BSc(Vet)(Hons) BVSc(Hons) CMAVA

Cats living in Australian households are among the luckiest in the world. With few exceptions, most Australian cat owners (or staff, as they may refer to themselves) keep their cats indoors most if not all of the time, feed them premium diets and ensure they are vaccinated and treated for parasites regularly. The result is that Australian cats are living longer than ever before, a fact I take great comfort from as a cat owner as well as a veterinarian.

It was my first feline companion — a moggy whose arrival in our household preceded mine by several months — who inspired me to study veterinary science, with the desire to extend the feline lifespan and prevent suffering the major drivers. As a cat lover I thought I had cats pegged. But relating to cats in a domestic context and engaging with them in a veterinary hospital are vastly different. Cats tend to be much more subtle than their canine counterparts. A dog with heart failure will typically cough, tire on walks and demonstrate laboured breathing. A cat with heart failure will compensate by reducing his or her activity — but may appear completely normal. A dog with arthritis might limp. A geriatric cat with arthritis can jump high enough to put a pole vaulter to shame.

One of the challenging things about cats, from a veterinarian's point of view, is their tendency to mask signs of illness until it is quite advanced. This was driven home to when I diagnosed my own cat, an eight-year-old moggy, with cancer. I knew something was wrong when she allowed me to examine her. Lil was not a touchy feely cat. In fact, any previous attempts to examine her had been met with a firm bite. She pulled no punches. So when she rolled over and let me palpate her abdomen, I knew something was wrong. As I discovered, she was suffering from end-stage cancer. Aside from skipping breakfast that morning and looking slightly unkempt, there was no other indication that something was wrong. I was able to administer palliative care but she succumbed to rare complications within three days. I was absolutely shattered.

Although cats can't tell us what is wrong or where they are sore, any veterinarian will tell you that cats are assertive communicators in a clinical context, and make it quite clear when they have had enough poking and prodding. Sometimes a tiny flinch gives away the site of a cat bite wound. I've learned over the years to take heed of a subtle flick of the ear or a slight turning of the head when I am taking a temperature or trimming nails. The majority of cats may be smaller than the majority of dogs we treat, but they are formidable fighters. The key is to never fight back: the cat will always win.

That said, even a cranky cat knows that we are trying to help. Owners are often stunned that their moggy is curled up contentedly in hospital with a drip in her paw or a bandage on her leg.

I constantly remind myself how difficult it must be for cats to adopt the role of patient. It is often said that 'dogs love people, cats love places'. This is true — the identity of even the most domesticated purebred is inextricably linked to his or her territory. We ask much of our patients by treating them in an unfamiliar environment, so we have to make up for it by interacting with them quietly and gently, taking things at their pace, and treating them with the utmost dignity.

Lil

My own cats have taught me much about what my human clients go through. I wouldn't have had any idea of how challenging it can be to fast a cat prior to surgery if I hadn't had to do it myself on several unforgettable occasions. Upon realising that breakfast was not being served, my cats started a relentless meow assault of car-alarm proportions, combined with performing extreme figure-eights around my legs to the point where any other activity but standing in the one position was rendered impossible.

I also know full well the struggle that some owners face just getting their cat in a carrier to transport him or her to the vet. Rest assured, being a vet doesn't make this process any easier. Once they catch sight of the carrier my cats invariably bolt to the most inaccessible location in the house (preferably in a crevice behind the most immobile item of furniture) and stay put until I am close enough to grab them — at which point they rapidly relocate to the next-most inaccessible spot in the house. (One reason that veterinarians have mixed feelings about house calls is that cats use this home-ground advantage to devastating effect.)

I continue to learn from cats, but one thing I know too well is that once you have lived with a cat it is very difficult to live without one. As if to prove my point there is a black and white Domestic Shorthair warming herself against the computer as I type. Unfortunately, there are many more cats than there are loving homes. Not everyone, it seems, is enlightened. The Cat Protection Society is one organisation working diligently to change this state of affairs.

When potential cat owners ask for advice I always inform them that two kittens are more fun and barely more costly than one — and two litter trays are definitely worth the investment! But I can't say it better than Dr Nick Trout, a US veterinarian who wrote *Tell Me Where it Hurts: A day of humour, healing and hope in my life as an animal surgeon*: '[Cats] are our seat belts on the emotional roller coaster of life — they can be trusted, they keep us safe, and they sure do smooth out the ride.' For this reason one thing I hope to see in the future is more nursing homes allowing residents to continue to live with their cats. There is nothing sadder than an old person — already rendered vulnerable by age and infirmity — being forced to surrender their beloved companion at such a difficult time in their life. We know that the human–animal bond is good for the health of both humans and animals in the equation, but we need to ensure this knowledge is implemented in policy that allows us to cohabit with our feline companions through all of our life stages.

Cats may not live as long as we do, but they don't judge, they love unconditionally and they give us a reason to get out of bed in the morning — and curl up in it at night.

In memory of Lil (2002–2011)

THE ARTISTIC TORTIE

Alyshia Hansen

Cats are like children. We make rules. They break them.

As far as rules go, my girls have life easy. Upon adopting them, they were on the bed within the hour. Two dark tortie sisters met one white bedspread. Did I care? Not at all.

Cat on couch, table or sleeping on my clothes? Not a word of protest here. Saffron and Licorice only need to obey three simple rules. Rule 1: no ripping the carpet. Rule 2: no sewing assistance required. Rule 3: no sitting on the paintings. Their adherence to these rules? One out of three. I've tried reasoning with them. I lecture them regularly on the subject. 'Yes, Licorice,' I'll say, 'I adore the fabric too but it would be better if you admire it from a distance.' Or when I'm more frustrated: 'Will you get out of it? I'm trying to cut out a pattern piece and I'd rather that the only slashing going on was where I actually need to shorten it!'

Then there's the painting. I paint in a style which uses generous washes of paint and therefore my canvas needs to be flat, not on an easel. That said, I use acrylic paints, which tend to dry fast. I sometimes even resort to using a heat gun to speed up the drying time to avoid feline accidents. However, every now and then, paws and paint meet. When they do, I hope that they have stepped in a little yellow ochre or burnt sienna. However I'm

Saffron

not usually that lucky. Phthalo blue is usually the colour of choice. This pigment has the staining power of mulberries, spaghetti sauce and beetroot all rolled into one.

Paws land in paint, cat is scooped up and swiftly deposited in the laundry tub.

After the frenzy that is 'cat meets water', cat finally escapes and sulks on the bathroom floor. 'Well, don't look at me that way. I wasn't the one who went and stepped in the paint. It's your own silly fault.' She'll then give me a look of 'Had I known you were going to haul me into the bathroom and drench me, I wouldn't have done it!'

Fortunately paw and paint accidents are infrequent. It's more common for Saffron to lie on the dry canvases. I've told her that it's going to be very hard to explain the cat-shaped depression in one part of the canvas as being a sculptural element of the piece. She doesn't seem to care.

So after several years, I've resigned myself to having cat hair in my art work. Perhaps it can be my signature. 'Hey, how did you achieve that texture?' I can always make it sound exotic and tell them that they're strands of saffron gently dropped into wet paint.

Postscript

As I was writing this, my mobile phone rang. I picked it up to the voice of my partner, a fellow artist and kitten owner.

'Pickle has ultramarine paws! I've tried to wash it off but now he has blue feet.' Trying not to laugh at the timing of this call, I replied, 'Hmm ... you might have to put him in the bathroom for a while to let him dry off without walking all over everything.'

'Oh he's already done that. There are blue paw prints on the toilet seat.'

EPLIOGUE: WHY CATS MATTER

Professor Barry Spurr

Professor of Poetry and Poetics at the University of Sydney and a Fellow of the Australian College of Educators

The numerous anecdotes in this collection give us many and varied reasons not only why cats matter, but why they matter a great deal to human beings from all walks of life, age groups, sexes and personal circumstances who have taken them into their lives. Often the cats have come from the Cat Protection Society but other situations are recounted, too, where the cats themselves have adopted their families, simply turning up on their doorsteps or (as was the case with my first cat, in childhood) having been dumped there. In these situations, without having had the attention of the CPS, the cats — often newborn kittens — are usually malnourished and require considerable time-consuming care and money-consuming veterinary services. People indifferent to cats or even hostile to them have often found themselves won over by a stray, and restoring the cat to health has brought out in them resources of compassion and commitment they might not have realised they possessed. Then they happily find themselves with a cherished companion who provides a lifetime of unconditional love and delight.

The issue of why cats matter cannot be separated from the larger issue of why animals matter, and this stimulates all kinds of considerations — ethical, moral, philosophical and spiritual; emotional and psychological, in terms of people's personal health and wellbeing; mental and physical; and the wellbeing of the animals themselves. Abundant research has demonstrated what every animal lover has always known instinctively: that living with an animal companion is good for you — physically, mentally and emotionally. Cats and all animals matter ethically speaking, because they belong, as we do, to the moral universe of sentient creatures. In our cooped up, sanitised and sterilised, increasingly urbanised and preposterously isolated worlds — where even the sounds of daily life (let alone the sounds of silence) are blocked out by ear plugs and other devices generating manufactured noise — our connections with animals assist powerfully in restoring us to what is natural and grounded in our shared sentient existence which, for most people today, is increasingly compromised.

Of course, as every cat owner knows, for all the immense variety amongst the feline population the particular species-specific character of cats touches certain definable aspects of human experience and triggers concomitant responses. These can be markedly different from those which dogs — as the most obvious contrasting example amongst popular companion animals — incite and excite.

The independence which many cats display requires a different kind of interaction with their human companions — and adjustment, if you are used to dogs — from the more available and effusive emotional connection which dogs usually exhibit. A number of the stories in this collection refer to the patience required in allowing a cat to express his or her personality, once confidence had been gained, and the ways in which cats can preserve a certain detachment even after their affection has been won and they know they are at home and in a secure relationship with a person or family.

But as soon as we start to make generalisations of this kind, exceptions to the rules can be quickly found, just as the assumed incompatibility of cats and dogs, because of the essential differences between them, is disproved by several anecdotes here; extraordinary harmony can be forged between what are supposed to be antithetical creatures. Moreover, in periods of my life when I have had two dogs together, one can be rather cat-like in her self-possession; the other can be what seems like the quintessential dog — spontaneously, utterly uncritical. There are cat-like dogs, and dog-like cats.

For these reasons I am always suspicious when someone declares, usually in an absolutist tone, 'I'm a cat person' or 'I'm a dog person'. Of course, differences in the species which determine the choices people make are perfectly understandable expressions of temperamental preferences, or even such circumstantial matters as preferring to have an animal companion who does not need to be exercised two or three times a day and/or is best suited, for example, to apartment living — in both cases, much better for cats than dogs. While acknowledging that we all have tastes for all sorts of reasons about everything under the sun, what matters, again, is to be an animal person. More often than not, those who claim exclusive devotion to one kind of animal rather than another are people who have never owned and been loved by the kind of animal they profess to dislike.

One of the principal reasons why cats matter, and the ownership of one or more of them matters, is that the relationship and devotion demonstrated make manifest to a world in which far too many of our fellow human beings are either indifferent to or display callous disregard for and cruelty towards animals; animals are creatures who need to be cared for and protected. For without care and protection they are bound to experience fear, loneliness, hunger or pain, or all of these. Moreover, unlike human beings — who can also have such bad experiences but can at least speak out to someone at some time in their distress and will, we hope, eventually be heard and relieved of their suffering — animals, being permanently voiceless, are totally at the mercy of whatever may be inflicted upon them.

The profound moral value of being attentive and responsive to the needs of any being is one of the gifts uniquely belonging to the human race. When we make connections and relationships with cats or any animals, these have the potential to enrich our contact and relationship with our own species. All creatures great and small have the ability to deepen and enrich our human engagement. This is especially true when children are introduced to animals early in life and come to regard them as a valued part of a human being's experience, and grow in an understanding of the appreciation of animals in their natural behaviour.

One of greatest 'cat poets' of all time and certainly of the twentieth century is T.S. Eliot. His *Old Possum's Book of Practical Cats* (published in 1939) is the main source of the libretto for the Andrew Lloyd Webber musical *Cats*, which enjoyed record-breaking runs on Broadway and the West End and is still popular around the world. Eliot's book is one of those literary works ostensibly intended for children, which is as delightful for adults. In the course of it, Eliot gives us a series of poems which describe various kinds of cats with delicious names: Growltiger; Mungojerie and Rumpelteazer; Old Deuteronomy; Mr Mistoffelees; Gus, the Theatre Cat; Bustopher Jones, the Cat About Town; Skimbleshanks, the Railway Cat; Cat Morgan and, most famously, Macavity, the Mystery Cat — and several others besides. It is all great fun, as well, incidentally, as being a brilliant display of poetic technique and of the usually serious, even solemn poet's genius for comedy. But beneath it all runs the essential idea that cats matter very much, for their distinctive and delightful personalities and for the respect and affection which is only their due as our fellow creatures on this planet.

ABOUT THE CAT PROTECTION SOCIETY OF NSW INC

The Cat Protection Society of New South Wales is an independent charity that has been caring for cats since 1958. We believe every cat deserves a loving and responsible home.

Each year, we help thousands of cats and the people who love them. Our services include a no-kill shelter based in Newtown in Sydney's inner west; discount desexing programs; welfare services for cats at risk in the community; information about cat care, health and behaviour; and advocacy for policies that support feline welfare and the human–feline bond.

We depend on donations and bequests and we're grateful to our members and friends for generously helping us to help so many cats in need.

Our shelter cats come from a range of backgrounds. Some are tiny orphaned kittens who've been rescued by a kind stranger; some have been well-loved, pampered cats whose owners have died; some are the victims of pet-unfriendly accommodation; some have been doing it tough on the streets ... some need complicated surgery and rehabilitation, others are bouncing with good health; some are pedigrees and some are moggies. Wherever they come from and whatever their circumstances, our staff, volunteers and vets give each cat the unique care, love and

attention they need until they find a loving home to call their own, forever.

Our work has been made possible by the kindness of benefactors, and the efforts of our volunteers, staff, members and vets. Thank you.

This book is dedicated to you, and to every little cat who ever warmed a human heart and to those still looking for the chance.

Cat Protection Society of NSW Inc
103 Enmore Road
Newtown NSW 2042
Australia
www.catprotection.org.au

PHOTO CREDITS

Cover – Josh Vernon-Rogers, 'Henry'
Front flap, top to bottom:
   Simon Hawkins, Kari Krall,
   Kari Krall
Back flap, top to bottom:
   Ashley Golsby, Kari Krall, Kari Krall
Half-title page – Kari Krall
Title page – Kari Krall
Page iii – Kari Krall, 'Jam'
Page 5 – Peter Toohey
Page 7 – Danielle Lyonne
Page 8 – Danielle Lyonne, 'Lorelei'
Page 15 – Judy Goyen
Page 16 – Danielle Lyonne
Page 19 – Danielle Lyonne
Page 20 – Danielle Lyonne
Page 25 – Josh Vernon-Rogers
Page 28 – Ashley Golsby, 'Buster and
   Lola'
Page 30 – Nash
Page 32 – Danielle Lyonne
Page 35 – Polly Rickard
Page 36 – Danielle Lyonne, 'Julius'
Page 38 – Danielle Lyonne
Page 44 – Tara Johnson
Page 47 – Danielle Lyonne
Page 51 – Kari Krall
Page 54 – Danielle Lyonne
Page 56 – Laura Kennedy
Page 58 – Adrienne Jansen-Howard
Page 60 – Danielle Lyonne, 'Joey'
Page 68 – Kari Krall
Page 71 – Allison Briggs
Page 72 – David Carroll, 'Mia'

Page 76 – Danielle Lyonne
Page 80 – Leonie Lai, 'Apple'
Page 83 – Nerida Atkin
Page 87 – Liz Pulo, 'Jess and Rex'
Page 88 – Liz Pulo
Page 90 – Danielle Lyonne, 'Shammy'
Page 98 – Liz Pulo
Page 100 – Kari Krall
Page 102 – Liz Pulo
Page 104 – Danielle Lyonne, 'Lorelei'
Page 108 – Mary Wolfla
Page 110 – Danielle Lyonne
Page 114 – Simon Hawkins, 'Piper'
Page 117 – Simon Hawkins
Page 118 – Kari Krall, 'Oscar'
Page 122 – Allana Flynn-O'Neile
Page 124 – Ashley Golsby, 'Lola and
   Buster'
Page 132 – Kari Krall
Page 134 – Paige Foley-Dunn
Page 136 – Phoebe Dunn, drawings.
Page 138 – Danielle Lyonne
Page 142 – Nikki D'Silva
Page 144 – Brad
Page 146 – Laura Kennedy, 'Schiele'
Page 150 – Darryn Rogers
Page 153 – Sam Kelly
Page 154 – Phil Blatch, 'Custard'
Page 156 – Phil Blatch
Page 162 – Julia Robins
Page 165 – Anne Fawcett
Page 168 – Alyshia Hansen
Page 173 – Bruce Diekman, 'Marvin'
Page 175 – Sophia Hill

ACKNOWLEDGEMENTS

The Cat Protection Society of NSW would like to thank all the contributors for sharing their cats; Chanel Stuart and Kristina Vesk for bringing all the pictures and stories together; Darren Kane for pro bono legal services; the team at Exisle, particularly Gareth St John Thomas and Anouska Jones; and the many others who helped to bring this book to life. Mostly though, we thank our feline friends.

First published 2012

Exisle Publishing Pty Ltd
'Moonrising', Narone Creek Road, Wollombi, NSW 2325, Australia
P.O. Box 60–490, Titirangi, Auckland 0642, New Zealand
www.exislepublishing.com

National Library of Australia Cataloguing-in-Publication Data:

Feline friends : tales from the heart / Cat Protection Society of NSW Inc.

ISBN 9781921966088 (hbk.)

Cats—Anecdotes

Cat Protection Society of NSW

636.8

Designed by Tracey Gibbs
Typeset in Gill Alt One MT Light, 10pt / 14.5pt
Printed in Singapore by KHL Printing Co Pte Ltd

This book uses paper sourced under ISO 14001 guidelines from well-managed forests and other controlled sources.

10 9 8 7 6 5 4 3 2 1